stemmy things

stemmy things

imogen xtian smith

Nightboat Books

New York

ISBN: 978-1-64362-150-0

Cover design by Somnath Bhatt
Cover art by Elias Chen
Design and typesetting by HR Hegnauer
Typeset in Arno Pro

Cataloging-in-publication data is available from the Library of Congress

Nightboat Books
New York
www.nightboat.org

for the girl-thems

contents

terrarium bimbo pop

true blue uncanny valley

life trance hacks mourning sound

author's note

Poetry both is & is not a luxury. Everything depends
on context. i, the author, am a white, trans, neurodivergent
person born on stolen land. i am a
worker, as well as beneficiary, of academic & institutional
assistance. As such, my privileges—invisible, visible
& ever emergent in my consciousness—
have shaped the proceeding pages. My intention
has been to trouble the worlds in which i move,
support, fail, live, struggle, love & continue trans-ing,
addressing with rigor the circumstances
that continuously shape me.

* * *

open letter utopia

after Audre Lorde

Linger with me here, from the beginning—we know not
each other's suffering, our specific subjugations. Every *I* after all,
born bloody, post-dilation, birth dowse, loose bowel, slip. Tell me,
who mothered you, bore your softness, bathed your limbs?
We come housed in hand-me-downs, our forebear's frugalities,
the wisdom of a seasoned pan. Do you find yourself
entranced with the by-&-by, dare you gutter, glitter, blink & lick?
Imagine my dreams, my kinkiest fantasies,
what i allow inside & won't, how reckless pleasure can be.
Tell me your words for gender—i need know them—
to see you, hear you, in all your splendor, now.
Hot for sound, mouth me names, speak *lavender, vibrator,*
coriander, pulse, hydrate, spectate, toothpaste & gush,
cuff my wrists leather to sky. This is what i mean
by *slower, right there, hold me down, now.* Listen—
i give you all my laughter! Poems for balm, for barricade
switch & raw, cobble ghosts in pressed leaves, pit fire
jubilee, fisty & clamoring *no freedom without joy.*
You need to know a radical touch,
that my *yes* means yes, my *no,* no, that yes & no
& maybe may shift while we linger, articulate, break
apart as moments ask. Does your blood taste iron?
i can't say, having never bit the bit.
Did you step from dream clear-eyed, cherry fleshed,
or rifle closets for dress in hem of secret pacts?

1

Have you come to terms with your femme cock, flat chest,
deep voice & spotty face giving something
you'd wish to keep away? Skin—trauma,
arithmetic, class. Rusty pipe bitterness, leaden, wet.
Will you let me be wrong, grasping at new?
We haven't got the whole picture, ask—for whom do you struggle,
whose block, whose street, whose power to say *enough,*
not now, no more, not ever, when—

ecologies

Like the dead-seeming cold rocks, I have memories
within that came out of the material that went
to make me. Time and place have had their say.
—Zora Neale Hurston

You wouldn't believe how lush it is here, everything
grows till it falls, nothing is trimmed or pruned, it's extravagant…
grows fast and then it has to stop for a while…
—Bernadette Mayer

deep ecology

I.

Gardens are for growing stemmy things
bending toward sun. We living sink heirloom
in tidy rows, set away days to brush clean
the stone, lay leaves that unfurl slow.
Nothing is ever finished—we are naked,
relentless, a now hard, now molten
presence. Some call this horror, others
beauty. Elemental i say, pieced together
of sky's generous weeping. It's fair
to wonder how earth holds our wreckage,
why we aren't swallowed in the belly—
though some questions answer them
-selves. You cannot swap a set of bones, nor
come from any other ruin than. We
gather days—dust, brick, bacteria, mortar,
form. Consequence gives a body
shape, says you cannot build home in a lie.

II.

i am not a woman. My gender is feminine.
Even the moon travels farther for what
it wants. Mostly i am water—swollen,
mourning, tie a blue ribbon round my finger
& forget me. Do you think me monstrous,
wanting my body my way? My poem
is a dream saying teach me where
you're brittle & maybe we can rest there,
where breath tethers limbs to toes
wrapped blue knit, where nothing alone
is useful. Deep in the quiet i touch myself
undone, stars still stars over turns
& brambles, a dark wood weaving beyond
city light. You love the mess, don't you,
the way consequence gives & gives—
stony dismay, a sweetness of rest. Here's
a poem for my body, stemmy thing—it
begins & ends in dirt.

so the maggots know

By way of explanation   i am
an unreliable narrator of my body
living gender to gender, marked
at birth yet far flung of phylum
straddling difference
between impossibility & lack—woman
& man—i, neither, though always
with children, a queendom
of eggs to the belly

O Datura—how we relate
abloom in shadow from the prying
sun's eye—perhaps i'm poison
sop bread run with bread
bleach freak borderline
kindergarten kid, poor dandy
fail-a-boy, nothing would stick—
not posture nor gate
tobacco cherries snuffed
in red pools on my wrists
        jump cut
to blue homely hillsides by the by & by
i'd sit, masturbate in laurel
thick with stench & moss gobbled
stumps for greening, dank leaves
& clacking branches

hard above—i, one small thing
unpinnable & reaching

My body, akin
to conifer—several
gendered cones though
you'd be hard pressed to notice
any male ones
through dense mess of fir & ash
the berries sprouting brambletide
in woodland hark, bower nest

What i want from levitation is a clear view
ways of speaking the here
i was or wasn't or will be
lovesick sopper upper left for later
a plague wrung holy vision
ask   why be anything other than
skin, racked taught or folding generous
about the bone, each organ glistening
groaning, chewed & wet
a priori even breath
we monger our hungers
to point of rifle—no no
no comeuppance for what pleasure asks
the femmy cock of me pouring
unstilted   sacred cup
saint silent in high tower, peering

Seldom the moments my own voice
laureli—sing a song of clearview
alive now   cuppeth run

Archive   my pplx
Celtic, strains of flesh washed pink
& prickle, northern beaches
mist bog & mountain thyme
their noosed language long aslumb, uncleaved
grandstanding stones for wolf moon
& cider drench, twist of globular rune
-raven thicket, the lake-locked lady
come sign o'er door
a gesture through   point way to-
ward Guinevere O emerald eyes
& multi-gendered woman, lake bottomed
translucent, barnacled
to murk—i shuck secrets
from oysters in the eyes
of elders who knew who wasn't
an either or an or or

Bb i am so unreliable it isn't even an issue
encounter me as mirror—
ancestor traitor to hetero indoc trauma
sperm drip hex then piss on my chest
my femme member hanging
underbelly   lambswool soft
like tree foot tarot man

eyeing the gap below, jucking

my great journey—to be split & split again

body to pavement thatching

opening more than once, more than twice

more than three times a maybe

fuck a doctor proclamate my body

as anything before a crown

You maggots devour sans differentiation

everyone oscillates   impossibles & maybes

morning catcall to chase-a-back

census tics, Em Dick's em dash a lusty

lantern writ every girl shines

o'er a potter's field of lovers lost

to night shawl & O—high lonesome

in rich peat we'll sleep

dead name giveaways

now ass sprouting dirt

dispersed tubular under moss

like beings formed of fungus

speech & rhizomat, fork tongue

birch sap, the me's of me

& you's of you, something

more than gendered coding

than rainbow window chains come June

or Joan's insolent man rags

burnt in loyal blue—true sister/

sibling, heed famine's warning

no monocrop, just listen—

every story feasts my her-them body
uncanny beside myself

Pplx say i'm dirt—i say we're all
barreling our way back into

these cadaverous times

Resplendent for all intents, an eternity of rosebud & leavened bread—
crescendo, heat, now rise again. The sun kneads rays over every acre
of skin, doubtless across the expanse. Never has the meat been redder,
more subtle & tender for the taking than in these cadaverous times.
Some things move like clockwork—vegetables & humans seasonally
uprooted, set against dry spells, sprinklered lawns, burgers, fries &
borders replete with jugs of punctured plastic welcoming the weary,
turned out from mourning according to their own whatever's-been.
We trust the text to tell us something truthful / truth-adjacent—light
like the life i'm in, or a dowry's just money for the man. In the garden
g*d consummates clay, throws gambits, grows torso, a head-full of
curly swell. Less is more fables spun Lilith, queen of asinine butt sex &
potable water. Another day in paradise, broke record gone gold again.
Picture Cain & Abel as lovers rather than brothers & the murder makes
primetime sense. *I loved him so much I killed him*, Cain claimed, thus
homo turns talented Ripley in the eyes of pious viewers. Civilization,
born of manly impudence, belligerent with its own selfhood. Lilith left
hers for the forest floor, rolling eyes shot with mirth. My criticisms beg
pennies—throw switch & unlatch zoo. Life in this time a grave cave,
souring where one shouldn't jet.

mother, mother

My mother is dead & the child in me grieves—
a stillness to the wind drifting slow across the creek,
tangled with skeletons of waterlogged trees. My father
phoned to say he found her—quiet in bed, middling
morning—one eye shut, the other, drooping.
i say next to nothing, numb inside & splintering,
having missed her final garbles—lungs labored
with spasm & twitch. Dear mother,

did you dream crepe myrtles & merry-go-rounds
as the tide sucked slowly out? i remain,
mourn your absence as if children
were your only life. Death itself was
slippery, roaming the marsh-line to find you—
flotsam girl, scared of new moons & lonely
for daddy's timber. i remember summer, crying

mother, mother, i don't want you to go — how you
smiled your toothy grin, hair spilling out your head
in clumps, skin edging close to bone. You
spoke gently, said *I love you* & that's all.
All i could say too in the end, having read
"Crossing the Bar," having read "Sunflowers,"
having sputtered my way through calls in a voice
unassuring—*Don't worry about me, i'm alright.*

The night, full of dark matter, distant stars
& satellites. She, released of toxin & phlegm,
soiled sheets, metastasis, the bitter & bittersweet
joy of her own volitions. Death beguiles—
you'll lose your mother too. Earth remains,
a shell against the clobbering. i dream
her now, tending hydrangeas as my mind prunes
our dull misconceptions—me, kind of woman
she never wholly knew, wandering the kitchen
on all fours, collecting scraps.

a kind of ripening

Body careen   consent to brush
        adjacent frames   ask inside & out

a know-how for motion.   i'm always
        a bit alone   in vor / textual

cosmologies of G I R L i'd emit.
        Innermost limb   worm virtue

-less soil for something richer
        mealier   even   than the boys

i knew mistook me   half hardened
        always ready to fake   (it)

for pleasantries sake.   Unbuttoned
        wish you would   bareness smooth

as moonlit paper   January dark
        draped overland   tangling

pube-like   among pine.
        i'm drifting into   thin air

finding direction   motions

      softening   a kind of ripening

fruit tumbling to ground   suffused

      below the surface   of nameable things.

Lonely mountain town

it's me again, come clean. i hid behind brown whiskers, whiskey & shame,
cloistered in girlfriend's closets from folk who'd clock me *faggot*
out F-150s, *hang your head Tom Dooley* stuck in their teeth. Camouflage
& excess, white lines & booze—everything inside me cardinals, prunes,
pulls a rosin gut drone to recollect. i say *remember bb, your first dress?*
Pink & pretty with blue lattice & curls, looking all Christina
from *Christina's World*, high country Carolina.   It was easy getting drunk
in leotard, laughing. Easy spending summer among laurel, forgetting
Laurie Foster, dead femmes drowned & raised americana.
More difficult to untwist the thorn, tongue jelly & cauterize,
divest from fear within. Could i ever be one of them—like that
woman i'd pass on King St., 14-eyed Docs & stubble chin,
rouge lips & black dress buying goth CDs on weekends?
          Not exactly—also yes.
Here i am, soldered together with Marlboro kisses, Vintage Seltzer
sober in floral print, alter for rhododendron & metro rat—swap
Brown Mountain for cherry tips, Maria Hernandez & chosen fam
bound deep as Hodges Gap.   Appalachia,
i paint my eyelids bluer than blue ridges so neither of us gotta look far
to find. If you see me out your window, i'm every name you spit—
friend, sister, brother, fag—clad shameless in Queen Anne's lace.
Find me staring up Bed-Stuy beeches, a bit of my heart back on Beacon
with the scrappy mountain ash. Lonely town,
i can smile now, remembering that first girl i knew—

warm at home & listening to The Cure. i dream a dyke bar
for every hollow, queeraoke sluts singin' Tammy off key,
highways safe for walking, ballads & barn quilts & string figures
claiming joy. i dream we dredge rivers & find no women there.

sleep theorem

Sleep is locational. Rest—a condition not exclusive thereof.

i was dreaming while you were—

everyone here   alike   deep colonial sleep   suburban come slumber
linoleum   phylum   things that fit   stilettos click marble   procession
to temple   shopping mall   Penny's Sears & dead leaves to bag   snow
days   home away from   moms exercising   power walking   shady lane
drippy spring   grill summer sprinkler then

no happy rooms no happy rooms no happy rooms no happy rooms no

The other night i dreamt i could forgive my brother—

Ability to rest is a condition generally associated with the settler
with   man   with   white.

You make your bed you lay in it. There is a bed
& you lie to lay in.

Sleep being a more visceral experience of rest.
A sleep. At rest.

The other day a professor in practicum made a joke about no longer
being able to make *those kind* of jokes. Approx 63% of the class   of the
earth   wanted nothing more in that moment than rest.

Do you hear so many poets   often white   often poeticizing their
awakening   post The Election?   Saying how tired they are & how
we're all like   gone totalitarian now?   Is this news?   you wonder   Is
totalitarian what happens   when settler civ devours its own?   Anyway
could you maybe use your library voice someone is trying to

Sleep is locational. Rest   something else.

i lit my candles   gifts from M & T   set them next my mattress straddling
floor   Lubed what seemed like my entire midsection   what felt like it
What was mine   Ran my hands   palms down   fingers splayed   bent at
three joints   gently   across my whole body   Fingered myself & fingered
again   Put the slightly larger than beginner's level plug in my ass & rode
it   no hands   or rather   hands   along my thighs   fingers pushing north
at perineum   fingers dragging over my little belly   mine   to finally hold
my heart   i came like that   hands on sacrum   breathless   at rest

Sometimes we play our coward cards, other times are like, legit tired. Are
there no happy rooms? Perhaps the ability to sleep through is conditional
on having never felt the question in your body.

What belongs to me?

Everything depends on body   500 years plus   how is sleep   or rest
possible?
   elsewhere   anywhere   everywhere

Friendship is a place of rest. Sometimes sleep. What's it look like to
thrive in states of crisis? We body striation. We body overlap. Impossible

friendships at the tip tip tipping point   of melting.

Friendship is so romantic.
i am broken i am not you are broken no you aren't

Please—

hold me in your arms
through raven dark. We close our eyes
to keep them

little spoon   big ladle   me   your tender arms

sweet poem

First time i saw girls like me dance together i stood root & gawked. Tough for me to picture ever moving that way, shameless & seen like sweat over celebrated—life itself post man drag & med. There i stood, question mark delicate as moth, wondering who'll nurture me as i sag—wilting we, big spoon spoon little 'til forever sleep comes. i never felt home with my only bones, only cock, flat chest tenor & top lip smudge—i learn slow & it's alright. Am i alone when my hands treat me hungry, guide my swells to verse? Some nights i lay awake, sugar-sweet as Amélie counting orgasms around the city—moans between brownstones swallowed by the Long Island Rail. *You're a rib of your own naming* i tell myself—try again to sleep.

They tire the role of boy to rupture. It's lonely thereafter—body queered in back seats, dingy flats, that one cruisy path wrap park to waiting wood. Today i make strength with my siblings, awkward tall & thick at center, serve brattiness with dishes scrubbed, breakfast fixed. i wanna be poached eggs dripping down a boo's lips, hydrangeas bluing the verge at dawn, finger banged & asked to stay over. Excess bb—too much paprika spicing the mix, a dash of salt over shoulder for every pinch in the pot, some disco lit fantasy sniff—

we let those other girls steal a look.

wild geese with transsexuals & acid

I.

It's true you should love what you love
Soft anemone
or hard as cock   limbo
like girl dick & constant letting go

Something scratches back my eyes   deep socket
exit foot arches   sows earth
rich muck   a basilica   every aching heartbeat

II.

My therapist's like *yr grateful for externals*
        friends   plants   poems   the hot pleasures of body
            yr feeling into
        this IKEA chair in which you sit   splitting at the vectors
            yet holding
        as body yearns for everything   outside of self
                            —So what about imogen are you grateful for
she asks & i mention   minus flinching   that i exist in queerness
        spiritual
            embodied
can feel move   act & touch from this   riverwarm
        whereas before i—   in the past—   ecologically speaking—

III.

there were me's who couldn't see this   suss'd
essence, some queer-ish things   but couldn't or wouldn't or didn't
       know how
to reach for & pull want within   saturate   satiate
       give name to my—

i used to get so drunk in the cut   walk home
nightly from the bar

(p a u s e)   4   (b r e a t h)   4   (m e m o r y)   4   (g r i e f)

it hurts what i have to say—how i'd sit in strands of cattails
by the highway 'n watch semis hollar by   hollar back valkyrie
scream-cry-think   should i *happen* to fall between their grills
none would be the wiser cuz my BAC's so high

IV.

Last night i took LSD   closed me eyes   SOPHIE'S "Pretending"
blasting   laughing joy at "Immaterial" transition   me
who often dreams of snakes   who loves to love their shedding
saw streaming light & neon slither   heard voices say

hey babe yr body's alright   yr bottom heart vast
its okay to be this   gay/ bae   soaked in gender

        tender w want—

flippity flop slut bimbo on pillow   fish queen   vitamin girl

just   this   queer   bod

V.

i can be so fucking saccharine
but hey   remember that Mary Oliver jam
          could be cringeworthy were it not so full of

You don't have to be one—

Just let the soft creature that's your body love what it loves
  here's my despair   now tell me yours
    meanwhile the moon   the sun   the clear pebbles of our thirst
      for EVERYTHING overriding—

trust me when i say through despair's an opening
it wrecks you wordless like foothills   mountains   more than voices
cities   trends   the quickness of sugar   ampheta drip   poems   skin
even the world that tries w all its human ways to kill

metamorphosis

A fish drowns easily in air—the body a syntax of flap.
i am nothing if not earnest, earthy, a woman spreading ash
over prayed-upon stone, sleeves of carnations to mentor
their tears. i have huddled in walkups quarantined with fear,
unwilling to love myself careless enough, reckless with joy
over spite for the world. Yet here is my softness outstretched,
my sourness borne through reams of abrasion, corridors
of unkempt rooms in this doll strewn flop of mind,
a sweet metallic tinge for all the body's de-postured
openings—its hungry loops & formal arches
trembling spasms of yes.

i grow verdant with run-ons & tiny breasts jutting
north like haunted mountains. Sometimes i'm woman,
all gibbous, pearl & jazz, languidly unfixed beneath muslin
skies, gathering secrets in mouthy eaves. To others
i'm always fish, so upended i hardly manage flapping—
body of peel, of missed connections thirsty for seconds.
The prick of desire fingers my ridges, flip flops atop
a belly gurgling Delphic till the drip spills out
like sloppy erection.

i wonder a dreamland of estrogens, turn from one
sort of birth toward other possibilities, bruised
& sparkling like a vein of stars. See flesh stripped

of grammar, ontologies of faggots in borrowed gowns
spun glitter with vibing smoke. i am a person
full of doubt & mirth, my heart tonguing envelopes c/o
you, You & YOU, a wardrobe of further interiors, vermillion
with angst, verse, smut, sex remixed & sprigging
tendrils down toppled walls. Nothing about the body is short
of miraculous—think cream-cradled hollows or sleeping
skin to skin. Think lemon trees in bloom with fruit or the line
in a poem where certainty breaks.

field jar

Every passion borders on the chaotic, but the collector's passion borders on the chaos of memories.
—Walter Benjamin

god bless the fire
which scours the filthy pot
—Wanda Coleman

field jar

Behind the red curtain, sun drips through. Radiator
adjust to three & books pile on sill. From the courtyard
a cat in heat & european squirrels color of foxes.

           Bell chimes echo, eggshell stucco, Turkic
      German swirl down Pannierstraße past kino, Lidl,
          Spätis along the canal, great swans, thermal,

coins & ancient shrapnel butting bank.
Midwinter dim & lust for pegging, dream cute queers
with stick poke skin, grass kisses & tulips on Tempelhofer Feld.

      i don't know what a poem needs to say—any penchant
         for narrative troubles me. i read a poem thatched
        with disparities, think real life's a jumbled-ass mess.

Group texts pass as lifelines
tethering time zones. JJ messages B & i
I'm in Delphi consulting the most ancient oracle—

      later *I am reading Carolyn Forché, & Sandra Cisneros*
      wrote a letter thanking her therapist, comparing her to a bruja,
        or the oracles of Delphi,

to which B replies *i love how folks before give*
us so much permission! and instructions!
& often i'm staring out the window at sun spill,

waiting on words to gather presence,

squeeze my nervous system edging the page.

Do i make poems to give myself permission?

To say *i breathe i desire i gender*

i linger here, over this & that, as long as it takes

to notice—? Is that a poem? Is this?

Whenever i read or write it seems i'm kneading

soft hours, flakey when i should be wandering or dancing

or getting up the nerve to go fuck a stranger at KitKat,

which could turn out kinda meh as both place

& prospect, but what's process other than choosing

between thermals or lace, wintering in line for the club?

The answer depends on where you wanna

land, one choice offering certain forms of permission,

another, entirely different. My favorite poems

problematize perspective, glimpse

acquiescence & it's these same poems that teach me

to write. *omgx i just ate the most bangin choc croissant*

i text JJ & B. *bangin.* Who even am i—

i never use that word! Doesn't it annoy you

the way white poets talk about THE ELECTION

THE HORROR THE UNFATHOMABLITITY of THE ELECTION
the ways we gotta to stay awake, stay woke, be vigilant—
some revelation? i'm like write a poem about the last conversation

        you had with your neighbor, your grocery list, maybe
        what you'd reach for in event of fire. The politics
        are front & center & you'll look less insufferable.

This poem comes to you from NYU Berlin,
an office in Prenzlauer Berg provided on fellowship. Later,
i'll sit at my table in Neukölln, sip Club-Mate & think

        about where i am, how i move with ease
        between Brooklyn & Berlin, Bed-Stuy to Neukölln & bb
        there's politics to that. What stumps me re

living in a queer body: maybe you feel
you can't survive in a given place because you can't,
so you trade that place for another, a city that saves you,

        helps you community, helps you connect,
        lets you work & walk & still get shit on occasionally,
        but largely, depending on intersecting factors, be.

But all the while, while you're being
(& you deserve to be, bb, really you do)
you're making it hard, perhaps impossible, for someone else

to keep their home keep their job afford their food
blare their music speak their
tongues—just be. Everyone who says a border is violence is correct.

All i do is walk about
with my field jar, look closely
for pieces of poems in debris.

B texts skeptical regarding verse. Warranted,
my fingers think. How to make a poem
that helps, that's not just a shiny thing, forthcoming,

a degree? Maybe the oracle knows.
Lick your finger, stick it in my ear.
i want the mouth of all y'all to teeth me

in your trashiest tongues.
Today's breakfast: three thousand miles
& currents of transnational air.

My heart aches for reaping.
Sun startles red through curtains. Cat & the yard, willow
green, pruned for envy. i too am a slut for spring.

here

You notice everything & want to live
in that noticing. Inside it smells
warm like pizza brick oven,
like café & coffee roast rising off
styrofoam, glasses steamy when stepping
inside, the car exhaust flanked
by Atlantic & the Long Island Rail.

So much sound—rivets loosening,
swelling when weather warms.
The downtown 4 angles awkward, sparks
tracks through Union Sq, metal on metal
like Sonic Youth in the '80s. To notice everything
& still wanna stay. Here, i mean
in body or city—this world. To notice

the bumbling stray fires everlasting. A trombonist
sliding their instrument to pitch, walking
straight up bent back as they blare—ways
of speaking. Speech is often careless, habitual,
another banal thing we do. You plagiarize a century
's worth of words & no one cares. People
make way with intention or no.

It's too cold for dice yet you throw
change for the pot. A lottery is
hope cast silhouette on poverty, wish lists
coded numerically. You notice nothing seems
easy yet everything's given. Nail polish,
ramps & bags of seed, a bottle for huffing
red lightning & pop. Frozen fingers,

crystalline, dangle off every eave. Ice
accumulates in vertical barbs. To note
is to know how water bears tales
of the rush. Molecules. The refinement
of osmosis. Open doors gently, feel draft
drift within. Beyond the sidewalk,
out on the pave, a soliloquy

of automobiles, mopeds & men
screech loud, the branch-lined parkways
laden with snow, bark flaking
like skin post burn. You notice
this & want to live in that noticing—
how everyone's already saying
everything there is to say.

leaflings

Dense time, Turkish coffee, sludge bottom, baklava. Today sits remnant a sweet tar enjambment—floss & spit.

The only way through is through & through is a-directional.

i drift the space of my sanctum—bedroom to bath, kitchen to commons. Out the window & four stories down the streets lay bereft as we left them. Wind ravages the March-soft roof, announcing in gusts beyond skylight & ceiling that the red wracked world remains.

It's an open question as to whether or not my bedroom belongs to me, my landlord, my plants, my dream lives & eroticisms, all plus more &—. When air quality in the borough's undependable, upon sun cycle & siren rely.

i arrange plants along my westward sills, small succulents & cacti first, aloe & peace lilies next, the rubber plant awaiting new soil. How verdantly they drink the light.   (snakes & zz's be damned)

Look—new leaflings uncoil. They—

which they, where?

—look up towards sun & moon, more directly at downtown Brooklyn & Manhattan, this paved up Lenape land. Desert succulents & suburban transsexuals—settlers either way.

There's no schema, mostly malaise, glitch, blur, a book half-read cuz the mind wanders so. i hang my earrings up each night, polish moonstone, rose quartz & selenite with chapped hands in tub water. Cairn rough shot, haphazard, place before the icon on halcyon days.

Screens make holy diagrams with saintly logics, sacred geometries, kinds of porn. A & K & S & B, each in their respective squares. Zoom zoom, check my hair—i'm up in the corner ready to read, the closest i've come in weeks to any kind of touch.

By 3 a.m. i fall asleep, pass the fuck out rather, my glasses on, stony baloney, headphones blaring Velvet Underground. i dream the streets downtown fill with queers, all the dead risen from this plague & that, reanimated to de-vacate the Lower East Side. i dream the feeling i get cum New Year's, walking from the F up 2nd Ave. for the marathon read, me in this mix of city & everything i know how to love, soundtracked in grainy Gretsch guitars from another time & place—Max's Kansas City, decades of junk blood unknown to me—even so, here i am, wake to sirens everywhere.

In this rose-pink room i masticate, swallow desire, coil & un—. It's just how hungry i am.

sunday morning malaise

do i just need to get fucked or is it something more
a human cannot live on iconic st marks poetry femmes alone
who says that i said that
if an asteroid strikes earth this century
some clever soul will project a giant meme across its stony space face
someone's sweetie checking out someone else's sweetie checking out
Beyoncé's natal chart & the people in their glass towers
wherever Williamsburg will laugh & laugh &
who can make a moral response
i don't care that Notre Dame burned but am quite interested in human labor
does that sound blasé   is language a temple
reading A's chap   words about writing about writing about the riot
books stacked at my bedside
Fanon yes Césaire & Acker   Cooper   Erdrich   Ess   Killian   Lawlor   Loy
Morrison   Moten & Qia Miaojin   Jeanette Winterson
Halal If You Hear Me   break beat poets my friends inside
very few things known   i talk a lot about
pinecones   floral arrangements
all my plants are phototropic & maybe i am too
somewhere many genders are rioting
for potable water   safe abortions   a whole police department's abolition
& so on & so forth & what does it mean not to riot with them
to support the burning from a safer space
everyone says a map is violence
i say today i'm gonna show up for me & me alone
though all the land is occupied

the other day i was doored by a Nissan & walked away without a scratch

sometimes the uphill path really can save your life

i mean slowing down

last week i sold the body of my labor   made several hundred   said ok

american money dead white killers in all our pockets

to believe in the trajectory of western civ is to believe the Greeks

were talking with rain-soaked Picts & Gauls   which they weren't

do any of your crushes know your name

are Medusa's pubes also snakes

i love that Velvet Underground jam but only on sunny sundays

when i happen to actually be in love   which is rare   which is why

i'm jealous of Eileen in *Chelsea Girls*   always in love always in flannel

today   get dressed for it   listen to Kelsey Lu

so what if we're both bottoms i'm sure we can make something work

Lenapehoking Pacific St. Crown Heights Bed-Stuy NYC

Richmond Chesterfield Watauga Dameron

Sutherland Skye Ancestry DNA the Surveillance State

i am lonely & come from somewhere

James River East River Gowanus Canal Riis Beach Atlantic Ocean

straits & narrows deep channel   i once witnessed lightning

over the Dalmatian Coast

am white queer monolingual born of plastic hi-fructose amnesiac

buy my femme dick a ring & shop butt plugs online when feeling kind

to myself   my belly slightly round   armpits musty as potting soil

B & P & i wonder when academics & admins will say *ya know what y'all*

    got this

but what happens once we're on that office window clean liquid tenure trip

these passion fruit seltzers are hella expensive

glass towers so high the neighborhood the nation

the Queer Nation the associations

litter & shade

i don't think literature does what nonprofit lit orgs think it does

& still i hope to win a Lammy

blue bell floral with trillium   hints of pink   several dollars per yard
    on Fulton St.

frontier is a myth a tar pit a suburb a café called outpost near my house

i wonder what pplx are thinking & how they can be so casually heartless

empath   i hypocrite   read sign & silhouette for filth in all my filthiness

make a list to share my asking—

what is a page   what is a foot against the pave-

shaped like a round

shaped like a pillage hole

shaped like a bread pan

shaped like insert card

shaped like i am gentle & don't wanna hurt anybody

shaped like blame the MTA

shaped like i haven't learned how to say what i want or am just too

shaped like a mess

shaped like descended from outer space meteor

some of us crashing all over someone else's beachland

it made me blush when S let me wear her pink FILAS at the reading

venus in capricorn i keep my mouth shut

everything matters but knowing this won't make you radical

won't make you a good poet & being a good poet won't make you radical

a pinecone is an organ either soft or hard & gendered by pplx in lab
    coats i guess

my body has no name

we see one another across a crowded space

it's priceless   sweet cuisine

please bring your poems to the riot

read & rally or immolate but show up nonetheless

i don't understand my language but the vowels are braced with anguish

body clocks

after Etel Adnan

All your life spent grasping at threads—less no ideas but in things, more just things as you meet them—clusters of ideation, spores spilling forth forming time. You're forever holding space for grief, adjusting to surveillance & deregulation, economic downturn spell spiral for the working class—sometimes poets too—everyone sick & strident chasing universal global health. You wonder how you'll live through this, bear body from bed to table, fork eggs runny while governor rambles—zone out, come back—splash tap to face & dream magnolias match your skirts. All the politicians say we're at war & the war is a virus much unlike other wars. You stare at the wall, ponder violence, the allure of ascribing valence to suffering.

Less than two weeks ago your mother died of cancer—cellular clusts of meaning made manifest & pioneering, ovaries to brain, metastatic. You've barely cried & judge yourself for that—must be hollow deep down, too familiar with loss. Maybe that sweet kid inside is just too scared to look. People will say she fought the good fight & the metaphor reproduces itself—song on repeat, cancerous cells, every body in various stages of decay. How does one keep from crying, what with day rolling forth like that?

There's a war on & the lacquer on your nails keeps chipping. Your new facemask is fabric of flower & vegetable taxonomic print—everyone getting feisty, letting eyes & brows do the cruising. You're hot for it, desire all contorted, a caustic squeeze snuck minus regard for social distance. Is this war? Were you ever alive in a time of not war? Manhattan stands phantom, stolen & gleaming, several miles through pane. Magnolias, hydrangeas, the rats down below, each pigeon & finch swoops close. Your muscles ache crossing kitchen, living room, climbing four floors to front door growing tighter in the quads, upper leg dull, constant life of decay. Hands cracked from washing, wash again—the fruit before eating, mouth with paste, doorknobs, toilet handles, dial on the bidet. Each surface a battlefield, a site for contagion, opening another state unstable.

The body clocks time & time drapes it, gifts shape, edge, contour. Renders time legibly.

You've returned to your room & it's warm there, plants & ambient sound, *Music for Airports* on Sunday morning, spring cum northeast. You slept twelve hours just to nap, tired of food & fighting. It's not for food's sake reflection sickens, leads cloth to shield from sight. Too much skin here, not enough there, this member at odds with heart head & assignation, desire lines white worming belly, thighs, breasts, teeth yellowed with coffee stain & cig. Nothing about your bones adds up, set against royal taxonomy. Surely, you ideate, a time of war. How novel. The usual has always been un—notation asks submergence, duration. Days prior were likewise quotidian—you'd walk to the A by way of bodega, dodge hollers, smell weed, opt this stop over that, arrive at work, school, library, park, the club with streaming bulbs & porous floors awash in human juices. You'd make it home somehow, circling back, text somebody *i'm safe i'm here*. Then as now you'd read words, watch porn, get hooked on the next limited run, pass out & tremor, note date, following date, scribble little phrases on a gridded pad.

Days echo—still. You stare at the wall, carry loads back & forth, room to room, two housemates & everything your body holds latent. This is a time of peeling, of slow reveals, themselves held latent for who knows how long. Amazing, you think, how the same things happen, slightly askew, war or no war, only there is never any not, any no, you know?

shimmering

i want 2 notice everything
    shimmy arms windmill & flip   my curly locks
pulled back 2 that tramp

                    oline palace   inflate

my friend A
       who's so fucking kind punk smart i wish you knew
    them /
we made classrooms 2gether   studied
all over   they said humans are capable of (   )

      we sat   sweating   staring
          at moon   full
over Houston in the Lower East summer
   you wonder why
   earth is
   like this
       everything shimmering & turning
       2 rot   why are you like this w
       your noticing
your terrible noticing
   & me—heaving
   wanting everything 2 stay
       in that place of feeling—

HOW WEARY WE ARE OF STRAINING

of banners & borders & books by men

ALL BODIES are
proof of desire   though not necessarily
tenderness   which breaks
a heart wide open

here i am in all my noticing   reaching through
throngs   & finding myself
finding you   seeking   lusting   holding—

babe   text me when you get home

year of the rat

Time is of the essence—essentially banal. Matter gains mass, hews as presence what moments devour, forms re-forming poly & ecologic from the get. Phases flitter queerly, evanescent & light. Tragedy, however minor, slips the mouth of morning, day upon day upon day, everything turning other, tangling velocity—your city, your block, 4:30pm & winter sundown cum night's descending jets.

i hope you get where you're going, that the state fails but pplx don't. i hope i get fucked today & that men on stoops, on sidewalks, up grocery aisles, park benches, in passenger seats & behind desks all cease their leering, let a girl walk home in peace.

It's like we've mined all hope from earth gut—we children, hewn of similar stuff. Often, it seems as if too much has been extracted. When i feel this way i wake, having not the right.

Time & being shift stormy, batter fences—say nation states, race & fixed genders—the unreal so utterly consuming.

*

The year chimes with a fury others will match. January—slash & burn raging, the topsoil a foundate for smolder. The world's all cinder & i get lit too, become one of those concerned citizens you see reading Hannah Arendt on the train—no shame, but it is a specific mood, a demographic kind of thing, speaks to class, privilege, white, as in we've hardly seen the beginning of demagoguery, didn't ya know? Performative outrage notwithstanding.

i'm unpacking my memory palace, cavorting with bacteria smeared ancient through gut, the pipes of my body, my city—here you are, arrived. It matters little what you want(ed).

History, says Hannah. *Fuck me,* says imogen.

*

What's on the tip of your tongue, bb? SMFGH

*

Several days since new year's & i'm blanking, moving content about the poem, seeing so many pictures of disfigured koalas in australia (stolen place), of kangaroos holding one another like children abandoned to nights of war—hoping for water & shelter, hostilities to cease. Do marsupials have a name for the root of all burn & is it Man, is it oh! Pioneers, is it Scorched Earth, dry & withering?

*

Comes a time. Comes a time when. Comes time. You & i & we & We enter time as bodies, an arrival's gate.

*

2020, barely January—did the president just start WWIII? At the time of my writing it's trending on twitter. World War Three is trending on twitter. #WWIII—battlefield Iran & amerikka's self-righteous bloodlust. i wish i were fictioning, that this was the product of some dystopian prompt but it's not. To paraphrase Hannah—the world's a fire & has been forever, yet i'm optimistic, despite or against history & better judgment, nature included. After all, there's lineage—Rosa & Hannah, Audre & June, Leslie, Jimmy, Muriel & Mahmoud—their syntax in motion weaving alongside us,

the language resonant, intact.

A person should listen to the dead, you know.

Die Toten mahnen Uns.

They remind us.

*

It's like queer utopia this decade or we're done. Like no more disaster capital, band-aid neoliberal or we're done. It's like no more white supremacy white history white property or we're done. No borders, colonies, illegal settlements or we're done. It's like fuck cops & armies & walls, fuck prisons & dilapidated subways, ableist architectures wobbling high over graves of workers & the enslaved or we're done. No more Clintons or Johnsons or Trumps, no more Netanyahus or Blairs etc., no handsome young premiers or sweet talkers to save us (poets included), like take a good look in the mirror everyone or we're done.

It's like civilizational clash east & west is myth propagated by popes by clerics by politicos (mostly men) over time is false or we're done. It's like pplx power or we're done, like pplx come together knowing we've shit to settle & redistribute, but first—or we're done, like realization of non-human autonomy or nope—canceled. It's like consensually fuck your gender fuck your friends masturbate with vigor or we're done. It's ten million things i could never name because of body, time, class, place, situation, right, —, get it? Whatever we do we might be done, but all my sweeties from Neukölln to Ridgewood are hot for mutual aid, dilating ring after ring & brimming electric, so even if we are we must act as though we aren't. Done.

*

Today i took a cab with driver K, one borough of Berlin across another to another, Neukölln to Prenzlauer Berg & several decades in time. *Seventeen years in Berlin* K said *& Moscow before.* He told me folx in Moscow were kind but the Germans not so. *Not even Berliners?* i ask *Not even Berliners.* Okay, this isn't my experience, but remember—you're stuck in your skin. In the year of the ox K hopes to travel to NY with son. *Come!* i say *the government is fucked, cards hard to get, borders shuttered because racists because fascists because Islamophobes & white supremacists but you know all this—please come! i will welcome you welcome you & many more!*

Me, an american citizen traveling by cab through the old west old east Berlin, through generations of ideas & temporality & rubble, traveling in a car driven by K, an Iraqi—it's 2020 we cannot be done there is so much work to do. In my heart i kept asking keep asking myself *imogen—how will you show up for this moment, this extremely human moment, right now?*

This. Now (collecting)—

In my mind's eye i see Bagdad & Basra, Fallujah & Mosul. Rocket flares on CNN. The president landing on warship like "Mission: Accomplished."

K drops me in Prenzlauer Berg. *Dive safe* i say. *Have a good day.*

*

Every day this January i wake in Berlin, throw open red drapes & say good morning to the yard, stare out kitchen window towards weeping willow, eat muesli & roughage & toast smeared Nutella, the grey winter sky sobbing slightly. Steffi plays Bowie other side of the wall & outside cyclists ding their bells, cars passing cranes along Pannierstraße where i'm gentrifier—white u.s. girl in Neukölln, a fact my trans changes nowhere—even as i feel so mildly safe, so utterly home. From where, again, have i come?

It's not a new feeling—you get that?

Who & what survives a colony, a diaspora, a so-called global community? Who & what survives the 15th, 16th, 17th, 18th, 19th, 20th, 21st centuries? Birds? Bees? What must we become in order to?

Say it again? On the tip of your tongue?

Thinking across distance—the greens & towns the Rhineland oversea to NYC south toward piedmont & Appalachia of my youth—i say gravely to no one *fuck that place—it fucking sucks. america* (stolen place), *violence, synonyms.* Sometimes one courts such thoughts &, feeling self-satisfied, pats their shoulder smug with privilege, all like *that's not me*— only it is, it is

& as Césaire has taught us, "Europe is unforgivable."

*

Every day awake i wanna be a flapper girl, wanna get fucked tonight by one, maybe two pplx of indeterminate gender, wanna dazzle myself with myself, lick rim, cum in my own face crying hard for more! Split me open bb, hex me out hard & make me quiver, make me beg & suffer. First night in Germany A slept beside me, borrowed my Sleater-Kinney tee, played big spoon. Alarms set, we slept till noon, ventured out & tried on clothes made us look all Marlene Dietrich in merino wool, ate 2€ doner. Everything covered in graffiti   RISE ROJAVE   Rosa wheat pastes   ANTIFA & Extinction Rebellion   radical sloganeering so dreamy i'm here for it—a real sucker for socialist imaginary. My phone alert says the president'll explode antiquities, says N can't get a visa but we have always welcomed nazis. i steel myself for minor humiliations, factored in as part my day—though it's only a child looks at A & i like we're faeries, smiling over their shoulder *I see you, I see you, hallo!*

Malice lurks but isn't the whole. i look at my phone & there's fire, look & see another man gets time served, look up at shop windows FREE PALESTINE scrawled bold, look back down & here's a cute date, a missed call from B as i trip over Stolperstein in platforms & dress, read names, dodge the tram, smell every bakery, take coffee, shop Lidl, still jet lagged & sauntering home. Who was the first to feel fear, to practice cruelty & why? Is it a particle gaining mass? It's banal, every last inch of it, the tidiness of cobblestone, the once route of walls.

i love being alive—is that crass of me?

Green headed mallards & swans, boxy bodies afloat on canal, bathe beneath bridges on Kottbusser Damm. Koalas front page the Guardian wearing third degree burns. Mustachioed men sip thick Turkish roast, smoke cigarettes, speak endlessly. Queers with pink hair & big raver shoes holding hands & i'm hot for 'em, wanna fuck them wanna be them. S brings me kombucha she made at Kottori. *Audre Lorde: The Berlin Years* screening at Kino, sold out but they squeeze me in. Grown men, manly men, all like *chowy! choosy!* it makes me giggle, genau? Days-old banquet near-rotting in the basement of Another Country where i finger through pages of water-stained Benjamin's, trans women in the next room dragging J.K. Rowling like *what a TERF! As-Salaam-Alaikum* across the weeks, i try each bake of baklava at Konditorei Al-Jazeera—pistachio & cashews & nothing's ever tasted so sweet. Silver Future for my 38th rotation—mocktails, bedazzled curtains, my friends Black & brown, Chinese & Bahamian, Indigenous, american & me— white gender fuck in Neukölln, Berlin. Thinking back to New York City, something of a Weimar doom about the place.

*

It's like queer utopia this decade or we're done. Like be radically soft & fiercely rad, in the streets in the bed in the class wherever you study, cruising park lanes & soul trains, the red carpet welcomes of one's chosen fam. It's like know your enemies—cops & bureaucracies spelling out policies held high in courts at gunpoint at cellular threat or we're done, capiche? Done. It's like save your seeds & share everything, repatriate land if you have it, tend a smaller plot or we're done. It's like anticipate PPE for the good of others, like shift your pronouns on the daily or don't, like cross not the picket line but yes, use you as barricade for bodies in history's way—i mean try to feel something about what isn't you, aka difference, the commons, the many, or we're done. Through. Like either / or is either over or we're finished & we can't be finished bbs—not while there's good techno to dance to in dark sweaty rooms, good drugs to take & water to quench us, friends to make & keep & process alongside, to fuck & be fucked by while surviving through to another coffee morn. Looks to turn, chances to take, years of trauma to shake through the sieve—!

On my birthday i visit the Garden of the Socialists & lie alone on Rosa's rosy bed, asking her how she kept getting over—over & over & over fighting day upon day upon day just to end up snatched off the street, bullet to head & tossed to river like so many women, like so many bereft of mass & ya' know what she said? She said *Bb, i am just one & you are just one & there are multitudes—our ancestors, our lineages & all those to come. Bb*—& this is what Rosa said—*bb, there is much work to do, so much work—*

we cannot be done.

terrarium bimbo pop

towards an economy of anal delights

If sodomy is sin, everyone here is criminal. Everyone
here, clit dick swole, pillar thick like Lot's wife
turned Gomorrah for one hot minute of lust. The anus,
ponderous, disapproving protestant ethics, a socialist
socialite labor commune—population: cum,
bacteria, bits of shit, occasional tears, lube love slick
& peachy for rimming. Let's play
ring-around-my-member, squeeze sphincter, pfft pfft!
Poems, pleasure, utopic gestures, useless
in terms of use value—like you can't buy a car
with them, can't pay debts or rent with them, wouldn't fight
wars over 'em, a hard enough sell on the shelf.
Seriously tho   aren't we all hot for change? i mean
grinding our teeth for it, acrobatic swing for it,
tied up & told what to do if that's your thing for it.
Imagine—August so gross, your sweetie's ass dripping
in your face like A/C units on a Lower East block,
swamp heat so human, hair lined spittle to cheek.
O, Penetration! O, Ambidextrous Poetics of Pegging!
Prodded like soft anemones beached on Riis,
hot & willing for revolution, meaning reevaluation,
meaning the world would look so different
if pplx with prostates knew what they were missing.
i do cuz i'm slut for it & you should trust me on this.
Let's talk about pleasure—asses spread, fingers
scrunched & turning, juice drink straw up my tiny box

& slurp. Here are the rules: take things slow—
economies grow steady & can always add jobs.
Smell my garden, amble sweetly, stay awhile
& turn the earth. You're welcome.

ants on a log

with lines from Eileen Myles & Miguel Gutierrez

i am always thirsty & wanting
to have sex. When you get
right down to it, a jar of peanut
butter works just as well as some
silicone egg—oily scrim
all smooth & creamy, mixed
thick w girl-dick spoon.
It's sweet, our picnic
like ants on a log, take turns
for lick & teethe. Ambition
-less i waste the day
think of you leaning into me
smoking, peering out
my window
as possibilities grow
& shrink &
i miss you, i'm glad
we don't know each other
cuz i only want the most listless
things, like crying after
cuming down crooks
of aisles, alleys
dunes—as sweet, average
& naïve as me—
bag of swollen skin

sticky sticky w cum
w fecal dirt soiled
& spread eagle upward
scumming for pleasure   first
as means   then as means
again

Like any woman's penis

mine drops down where thigh slaps thigh getting sticky
with summer—that warm salty wave welling up up up.
In this way i differ from some woman but not all—a matter of kind
rather than degree. i pedal my bike beneath moonlight through park—
no branches but shadows of branches, a few pesky stingers maybe
cruising in the thickets. Virgo season hard lean & glitter smear
cheeks riding no hands like Hunter Schafer—there's a girlhood
i need to give myself, late 30s, licking wounds,
done counting bruises my body holds. Anyway, fewer
than belly laughs notched with J, smearing lip stain at Sephora
like we fear no germ, or that slim bit of power i get
hollering *fuck off i'm my own girl!*
Greater than the possibility of breakage is the dream
of a whole fist (at least three fingers) or a stately purple strap
-on loving the shit outta my earthy ass. When T said *leave the chain
take off all the rest* & came down on my wrists like Sappho on the rocks.
How extra! What a miracle! i dream in Fenty, a friend's HBO, mostly rigid
silicone & late '80s mid '90s smut. My nightstand, painted pink with aloe &
gems—moonstone rose quartz star cluster garnet calcite orange blue—
pinwheelie sex toy like some medieval Joan of Arc shit & a dog-eared
copy of *The New Fuck You*. Sometimes i feel like a caricature
& in this way am like so many women we know. Like any girl's penis mine's
average because i'm average & usually date pplx who don't shave their pits.
i'm a woman who doesn't shave their pits but does shave their legs
because i live to laugh at my own sweet secrets.

red dirt garden goth girl

fuck me down low in the lettuce patch Diane   fingers to earth & ass in
air   my heart ain't nuthin' but a rusty trowel   strong enough to break
horses   darn socks   knit quilts   love hard & sloppy like blackberry
jam   all kissy kissy 'bout our lips   there's nothin' sexier than fucking in
the dirt Diane   our boots muck stuck where we pulled out   Wranglers
chucked across a rotten bow   lover   maybe there's no tomorrow   so
till me deep & rail me good   use that rose quartz dildo & harness like
a she-mare   vegan leather pony trap   i'm just a red dirt garden goth
girl   crooked halo high on hog   paper wings & dulcimer strings like
chains around my red sun back   why o' why was i ever born   but to
be some futch's faggy girlfriend   limp-wristed   never bested   handy
with poems & pruning stemmy things   a regular rose of sharon bb   do
with me like the bees   say grace   sticky sticky till i'm pleased as peonies
you droolin' down my creamy folds   i say my heart ain't nuthin' but
a rusty old trowel   handed down the dirt daughter line   our names
sound round the hollar   knockin' backdoor barns & sheds   flutter
flutter   cardinals brown & red   hoverin' past their prime   them girls
like me   we dangle cock   we splish splash   up in the hayloft with the
devil   sweet talkin'   long dark blues & will-o'-the-wisp   talk to me
sinner   say my name again   told ya 'bout the time me n' Jolene got
busted   saturday night   swamp country   asses up & out the trailer   we
bolt ran   shared a laugh or two   popped yellow jackets in her beat up
ole tacoma   highway 40 split north 95   i'm a city girl now
                                        but still know my own name
sing it with me Diane   somethin' outta shape note hymn   concrete &
barbed wire concrete & barbed wire   just a red dirt girl abidin'   spite

beatings & boredom   the bulbs of despair   out-foxin' Tom Dooley
'neath a rave talon moon   why o' why lord was i born this way   girl
not girl in Deadhead dress   singin' where will i be when my trumpet
sounds   o' never mind just fuck me down low in the lettuce Diane   let
me feel that red old clay   home place stuck 'neath my nails   i'm a sweet
girl really i am   just a sweet Opry girl   wreckin' ball   wanna do right
but not right now girl   tar heel bastard bitch state line or bust   ruby
fruit kinda girl's girl   gathering moss in my husky basket   hitchhiker
east Tennessee truck stop trinket   slash-a-tire for Laurie Foster type
a' girl   eat Bo-rounds & Cheer Wine to pray the trans away   hee haw
yee haw   my bush smells like campfire   kudzu danglin' round my little
titties in the backwoods type girl   Waffle House angel hoardin' quarters
for jukes   Garth on box like I coulda missed the pain but why o' why
just give it to me smothered covered & buttered Diane   hankerin' for
fuckin'   back seat of a car   slash killer drive-in like uh-oh   uh-oh   stay
weary that side a' the mountain bb   live another 9 to 5   lazy sun cruisin'
round heaven all day

                        i'm just a red dirt garden goth girl   would
ya shut up & love me   unconditionally   storybook bound & stinky pits
string figures & Winston fits   bristle face & cock tucked under   cast
iron cobbler   chocolate chess n' chitlin' smolder   takin' sober-ass walks
through nighttime glen   O Diane   never will i ever drink whiskey again
Car Wheels & Lucinda spinning speakers at 3am   high on cheap speed
& Kentucky Gentlemen   veins aloof like to o' why me   lil' sweet pea
thirsty for the great mosquito let

winter voyeurs spring voyeurs summer
(eat my skin)

Isn't there somebody
i mean anybody
wanna make stupid eyes
at me? Asking for my double
doppelgänger   inner twin
umbilical in their ability
to read me prior
gesture   prior pen.
i'm out here in my dumb
gay shirt   all tie-dye
& cropped   little dark
cum spots dot citrus
prick & burst.
Where belly
crescendos beltway
that's my sweet spot.
Go wild when ya drench me
there. My other's a little louder
than me   braver   she's shameless
sings peach tunes
from the hammock
on our rooftop gable
greening
sweet bud who never tucks
& rarely thinks twice

re sucking in public.
They want adoration w/out
U-Hauls or winter cuffs
what homely dykes call
impulse these six-foot sick
mask days. Yr girl wants piss play
   like long streams
v hydrated   straight gold
arching dick to gracious
face   rainbow-esque oil slick
maws puckered for Os.
Natural comeuppance
these glorious strands of pearl.
Who even needs a showering
April? Asking for me
my friends & any won't-be
suitors hollering *bitch*
to my back on the block. Follow too close
& she'll bite yr ass
while the snacking's good.
Just skip me like flat stones
to June as in spoil me
marvel me   ruin me
darling you ain't the first.
Rope or lather   finger
thrust'll do—take
yr stupid eyes & smoosh 'em
all over me   outside &
midday in a crowded park
   preferably.

i'm not upset yr upset

Look—i get yr upset. Must be hard
admitting you've been wrong all this time / extant
universe being literally unfathomable now here
you go crying autogynephilia, psycho-science pseudo
faith un-fray me. Hate to tell ya'
i'm a true girl after all / no god no man
no 2nd wave claim or boy wizard need fix

me. Suppose you expect i bury
a cross beside this axe i'm grinding,
men like you being martyrs & all. O you
w penis who feigns deigning penises, why on earth
do you hate yrself so? Girl / cock, delirious,
so angry when confused—nobody
told you so? Darling i'm no bimbo
sans my say so & since i'm the one speaking

get this: some days i'm happiest on drugs
reading poems   having sex
   rough   choke   slap   fuck
though it's nothing to do w you / i won't
give myself away just bc you claim
to thirst. What a complete fucking monster

you'd make of me, yr bright ideas & birthright
grinning, the teeth all buck in yr head.
Newsflash bb i'm a 21st century girl / not
some Jackie O replicant pink suit-turned-palate
for boy-brain oinking up my shimmering face,
capisce? Admit it friend—yr upset i won't swallow
it tooth, line, another girl gone sinker / but
what's femme in me's been warped

from the get. Guess you think i hate myself
too but its hard admitting yr wrong
every time. When my body feels dandy
i pang prick & hunger—rouge lipped
w darkening brood staring dead in yr eyes
like Lauren Bacall   blowing
nasty ass smoke from my nasty ass Parliament
right in yr stinking face / prerogative being
you can love me like you love me when you love
my mine alone / when & where & how i ache
for it or literally just go the fuck home

nicotine libidinal

It's rude to speculate over someone's gender but you can't take Kurt
  from the girls
We pair plaid   skirt to boot   get on best w babes like we   fuck-all angsty
  in bleach bloom
jeans   shredded tees   superfuzz big muffs like give us everything
  louder than—

Red rover red rover about a bb girl cum over   Long before answering
  my body's call
there was Kurt
                scissored out guitar mags & tacked to my wall
Kurt
                screaming nicotine libidinal gravel
lil' Kurdt
                endless nameless   black candle set w stargazed lilies
                mothy cardigan   ugly dresses   blond-pink roots &
                wispy extensions   eyeliner slop   like the girls learn do
                collage doll parts to exorcise   née entertain

Remember our girl w his boys Krist & Dave   dude in braided pigtails
bobbing 1992   main stage Redding singing all my words are grey   Fucks
me up to hear it cuz i know what he means   what he wants to say—
says later   In Utero closing   can't get there yet   —i mean c'mon   have
you ever read the liner notes for Incesticide

like hey all you sexist   homophobic bros   fuck out
-ta our shows & stay away
Nobody loves queers that much who isn't

Idol friend   sweet cadaver   breaking strings & toms   love you like an
Aerosmith cassette   worn touch   reach through time   image   snarl
sound & vision   Touch me here   on the sickness i mean   It bends us
back like questions—   sores our stomachs too   i pray for rest   K sleeps
w angels   happy as chorus   cuz all alone's not all   we are   Didn't
Courtney put it best   when she   when we

        fake it   so real we're beyond it

(fake)

                                        a way of saying cisgender

    revelation like aneurism   louder than everything else

every pearl's un-insides (feat. poppers + feels)

I. *It's Okay To Cry*

i've always had a rough time crying. When my mother died in spring well sure—i cried a bit, only not as much as you'd imagine   sirens running up & down Atlantic all night   that year's death spilling into this.

When i woke on a January Saturday to news that SOPHIE'd passed, my first reaction was something like *faaaaauuuuuuuck*—syllables drawn in lengthening waves of sudden grief, undulating, looped

& that sonic response was followed by the thought that yes, of course SOPHIE died   last year's death slipping over into—.

Since their passing in the spring of this January i've thought a lot about the girl woman faggot enby   who / whatever i am   how she never really got a chance to know them. My mother. SOPHIE.

II. *Ponyboy*

First of all—lolololol i fucking fuck w this song it fucks w me back   like who says a eulogy can't be joyful <3<3<3

There's a bottle of poppers beside my stereo [No New York + a handful of R.E.M., Sonic Youth + Mariah Carey discs] i just opened—twist cap & sniff standing   mid- afternoon lukewarm   my face   felt it reddening everything inside turning soft   bottoming   squelching static belches

through dark matter   cosmic FISTs   i sink in oscillation   post-Adderall
& hairy sativa

good god pony boy   pony pony boy   bb's just a pony   boy (?)

III. *Faceshopping*

for genders at Atlantic-Barclay mall. If you could buy a new face, what
would you do with the old one? *My shop is the face i front.* Wow—
poppers got me all relaxed, whole body like dog jowl oozing, brain on
down till my organs cum liquid, sludgy smooth.

Around 2:16 into this jam & all that was / is me goes puddle—green
wispy tendrils leafing at the edges, flies & also butterflies imply stickiness
thick & wandering—pooling magma to root.

O wait! O fuck! A jolt back to shop—my face is the face i front. It's
possible to make presence in your body but hard to sustain the effort
legibly. Like, my face is real when i cum but i've never seen my own O
face—have you? Maybe it'd make me cry or wanna climb into the moon
like SOPHIE—such intimacy, tie a blue ribbon round my member &
forget me.

IV. *Is It Cold In The Water?*

When she went up to the moon & i knew not only was she gone but
understood that that's where she was headed all along, where any
number of us are destined to go & rest with each other / from each

other / alone or more likely in some configuration beyond imagine—
from there cums Is It Cold In The Water?

i see SOPHIE soaring a-directionally in slo-mo & think of bb imogen
in their suburban bedroom—a kid listening to *MONSTER*   hearing
Michael Stipe's voice   how it pierced my skin like drug-dipped nettle
opened veins lakeside to moon & now other girls like me (girls of every
gender) on their backs on their floors tonight   doors shut eyes shut
pretend world floating pretend world floating pretend world leader
sure   i've a soft spot for pop stars when they look like how i want to
want & be wanted.

V. *Infatuation*

Never overrated. i want to nap in an emerald forest of futches from the
set of *LEGEND* where everything lives & lives. That's what this song
sounds like—napping through a Ridley Scott banger & i wonder what
gender i'll wake in.

i listen to the beat of my heat, happiest on the floor, feet to fours, the
lights spinning out as sound drop-throttles spine chord to core. When
i dream it's not all night terrors or sampled electric guitars but a dainty
figure i've been chasing since my youngest boyish girlhood—they know
every willow bend & speak with forest creatures tonguing weird, jazz-
time syntax back & duh—i wanna understand.

The moss gets me wet as *i wanna know* reverbs w trem.

VI. *Not Okay*

Hole stratospheres made of squashed frequencies. Sexuality blown out snap snap snap   everytime. This song scares the grown-ups even more than Nirvana—

   if only Kurt had lived to sophie.

VII. *Pretending*

Making trans- out as something spiritual   i don't know, for me it is—i feel full-bodied herein. Whatever i say says so little so   come closer unlatch my sound + vision.

i'm hesitant to write about it in spiritual terms because every dumb fucking thing a trans bimbo thinks becomes a statement in its time & i'm just a wreck of a girl with some poems they'd trade for any chance to get spun   dance skin to skin for skin for hi we're all here in body we survived.

Imagine the full sky blue with moon prowling through day. That's your temple, your sepulcher, your holy shrine opulence & opulence fills you, even if only with something you're playing at   alone in your bedroom with thrift skirts & memes   meditation   a pinch of astral projection & salty-gossip prayer. You wanna be spacious, safe & FUCKING SEXY, want a dick & tits & ass & open   wanna suck a boy's vulva as you drip drip drip ever sloppy &

here cum those sub frequencies elevating again to the wide-open wash of euphoria—drug & it tickles the throat, relieves & right there's your god   your gender   this is the song that plays & maybe the title is ironic maybe iconic you decide.

VIII. *Immaterial*

Blood on my jeans in the place where i—

People hate trans folx & queers in general cuz a vivid imagination plus body makes body somehow more than material

which is what i think SOPHIE was angling for the night SOPHIE went away. Something more than—

A song / poem can be a dwelling where freaks cum for dreaming. The thing is—it feels so hot in that place, so fucking   g o o d   like you could stay forever but then you'd betray it

betray the liminal when you lock step inside.

Capitalism is catching up with us. Life should be easier but a proliferation of manufactured ease / gender will only erase our elders &—

IX. *Whole New World/ Pretend World*

In the end which obvi isn't, SOPHIE is really funny really sweet really earnest & it takes a special person to pull off so much cool. i wrote this as an excuse to get fucked up & have a moody lil wander—to make something expansive from a grief that's partly SOPHIE's, partly the plague year's & partly bb imogen's, hungry for a SOPHIE to look to.

Feels lonelier here than even before—its like when SOPHIE passed a chip got chipped off the Dark Crystal & now everything's less horn-smut, joy askew—can you hear it—?

In sound i sense utopia like even when somebody dies they keep going—our blue one pink with wolf moon waxing.

desire goes nowhere but somewhere sometimes

I.

The light is softening. We can laugh now if we want, snug in
autumn wool, Docs laced & tacky tights, drink bubble tea
on 2nd Ave. Everything i remember, turmeric & banal, that time

we went for went to went—. Desire goes nowhere
but somewhere sometimes. i'm Rooney Mara in *Carol*,
pleated plaid & beret. You can be whoever you want—

there's no better way to live. Roaming blocks of scaffolds.
Lack scaffolds you're not in New York—stonework
crumble, flesh glass & steel. Difference undoes us, albatross

& wash away. i come from down south & my skin is white,
raised boy but no. So gay i can't even walk straight—
that's B & i's little joke. Never was i ever Larry Kramer,

lecturing a field full of queers.
There's history & then there's our histories—silence
or reckoning & what will you choose?

i'm the woman with a whiskery face, chipped nails
& girl cock dangling. All confusion is mine—my cherry delight.
Reek with me bb, slip out all the air. There's no better way

to live. i'm Diane in *Paul takes the form of a mortal girl*, marathon fucking, dawn paint splattered bibs to set the dogs free.
What would it feel like not to hoard anxiously over

tomorrow? Is your heart okay, dearest? Is your heart
a pumping, fisty, blood-plumb thing? Now is always
the time for crying. Our tears make us look like

the fierce-ass femmes we are. One night, it was summer,
a man spit in my face. All i could do is keep walking.
Keep walking is all i know to do. It ends well cuz

here i am, writing you, musing after Lou Reed.
Behind every snotty boy is a Rachel, a Laurie Anderson.
Behind Christian there was always imogen—

my own ride or die, my own Coney Island baby.

II.

Desire goes nowhere, feels like somewhere
sometimes. The city exaggerates—an armrest mid-bench
to thwart sleep, gingko droppings & boiled nuts, oil slick cum

stain trousers unwashed. At Doughnut Pub i flirt with the server
who always flirts back. Tall, strong hands—we're of a kind.
STAR House was located at 213 E 2nd St. Marsha & Sylvia

fed & raged, sang outta key pop tunes with pplx
like us, or pplx far removed from, or pplx like both &.
Difference entangles, scaffolding everywhere,

please bb, braid my hair. In the soft light we laugh—all we do
is walk is talk is hold hands totes dreamy—we of some kind,
trying not to notice the John Varvatos standing in for CBGB

as the city conflates tit for tat, paves over graves. i'm so lonely
i'm never lonely, cruising Christopher St. piers aren't we always?
Peach says they're the Widow of Summer. It's true.

P is called Peach & i'm breaking my own rules, names
in poems like who even am i Rachel Zucker? Pplx just dazzle
do they not? They do. i pocket lipstick at CVS

& never wear it—does this increase my chance
for smooching? Sometimes in secret i frequent Cubbyhole,
drink seltzer like a normal girl would. Sometimes

i stalk Union Square, suss sight of the Factory
where Valerie shot shot that Andy nearly dead.
Soft reveal—i'm a lesbian separatist deeply invested

in SCUM. The heart—what a curious, hunterly thing.
Have you ever seen the double dutchers double dutching,
the dance-offs the greetings the drunks the Friday night

wonder of it all? One night on 2nd Ave. some medics rolled David
Wojnarowicz away. What remains is timbre—his anger his lust
his long drive dreams & voiceover tapes. Now i'm dressed

like Rooney Mara, only actually gay. That's our difference
& difference makes us. Maybe i ruined everything saying *i've*
the crushiest crush that ever crushed on them right

before they dropped me at the airport, but all i can do is
keep trudging—every situation dissimilar, fleeting,
chasing some pheromone some garbage slut lust.

III.

Desire, even the light is softening

Remember the fountain where we almost kissed?
Cute selfies snapped waiting for the A? The time
we watched moon rise on the median at Houston & 2nd?

Remember? STAR House was located, is gone & there's
two statues of binary gays painted white in Sheridan Square.
i saw *Julieta* & *The Handmaiden* at Sunshine Cinema alone

& it's gone now too—bulldozed, make way for blank blank & bank.

B texts *meet me at Happyfun*   corn dogs & soda bitters
all spilly spilly with the tea. If nothings erotic, no yearning,
utopic, we say we don't want it—girl-boy-them count us out!

Life gets heavy but what doesn't. All we can do
is keep walking, desire going somewhere off kilter sometimes.
Dawn flares as skies azure their Lazarus swing—

reset bb i must be dreaming—Us & us & us

spooning in sheets of filth, our tenderness held
secret from the world. Be whoever you want, there's no
other way, believe me. Dirty feet, scratched backs, sticky

bellies & light sharpening as street cleaners do their thing,
everybody honking like come the fuck on & get over.
Morning breath mingles like rubble & jasmine tea.

i'm some ghost girl out the grave in a dream

of scaffolds. i'm the runny eggs dripping
down your lips—you can be my bossy top & me
your bratty femme, bite your fingers as you fuck

me from behind, sounding off loud cuz
who you think's in control? Look at us—our suburban terror,
banality & glory holes, leather beauty whipping

ass with some splayed thing. Hungry. Greedy.
Beat me into morning like everything else.
We forgot to wipe yesterday's makeup away,

as if tomorrow were guaranteed & we, waking, already

had a foot in.

true blue
uncanny valley

*Our skin absorbs culture and its hypocrisies as it navigates the earth
and the weirdness of time. But it is a dreamy packet
with golden strings dissolving into the other world.*
—Fanny Howe

*Water brings energy the way memory creates identity.
All I can tell is that I was here.*
—Etel Adnan

Morning & the egg slips from shell. Colombian roast grind cylinder, aroma sweet like hint of caramel. i enjoy a yolky mess, the way it spills beyond white dimensions, swells runny in space. i want to live like this— ruptured shell oozing cross a cast iron archive, accumulating tastes.

i could go anywhere—skip, laugh, burn away, shake ass shimmy— nothing the same way twice. Look close: does it feel wet, iffy, a bit sticky, wild like the times when

Everything reflection of refraction of cinder, once fire once kindling once sapplingly green. Whatever i know gets (re) learned daily—rent wide with breakage, tenderness & retrospect.

The more we talk the more abundant we get—also fissured, turned around & split. One encounters a Many—ashes to saplings becoming with. It's molecular, environmental, all sex brought to bear. Arms, oil, the empire bit by bit. What isn't always bursting at seams?

Can anything ever be beautiful? Adorno says something like poetry's barbaric after Auschwitz. i say what about post-america, 1619 back to 1492 on—this ever-lengthening list of names? Stolen lineages, stolen land, stolen labor, stolen languages, stolen kids, stolen blocks, stolen breath, stolen.

Like here it is! Here lies the Holocene! How temperate it was till cinders smoldered, sparked cruelty, burned toast. Easy come easy go i guess— Will Smith socking that alien

welcome to earth.

So much life is walled away, dying. Sit with things & let them speak. A thought holds space for other thoughts.

i feel madness root sick within. My ancestors—north island shepherds, knot weavers, cairn builders, lake ladies swapped for myth & smithy, turned colonial, famished or both—appropriators even still.

My ancestors—sustained through ecologies sustained through death. Peat diggers, carbon-born bog men pressed flat, necks snapped. Where did my pplx learn the rope?

O prodigal children of earth, no one doubts our albatross save we. How account for what's been done? No rest for the wicked, white as bone they say—this euro-merican descent.

Nobody's one body, never someone minus many, this goddess stitch ecology where nothing's owned. My body—gendered skin, class(es) of motion moving through me, the heart burning brightly against

i am a soft syllable my ancestors never uttered, a tone eluding their conquering tongues, leaving them fallow, yet speaking—how language holds hostage our worlds of intent.

Refusal is not romantic. Pick a scar & shovel. Haul harvest to another's table—we kin with our work cut out.

Today's word is abundance—a kind of practice, voyeuristic & pronoun-free, analog verse yoke lineage, favor & lack, whole boroughs & mountains made grid—stolen, sold, handed down & sold again, commodity plus market stooge i was, i am. But enter me, other, embodied

—blossoming orifice & hungry sheaths of skin,

neither mother's daughter nor father's son but something else entirely. The doctor interrupted my jaundice wails to assign privilege & point of view. The rest of the story goes me, interrupting interruption—slowly learning i must, i can. See my sinews barely holding, blotchy lungs healing, a kind of pink within—perineum throb, thirsty for pleasure, for unmapped phylum, genus, canticle—winded from all the gasps & gagging. What we'd be with all shame stripped.

K says we're all A cups till proven otherwise. We laugh at the boy poets trying hard at being boys. B tee-hees, i lament, motion toward the plateau of my chest. With less stubble, a hint of breasts, would pplx take me seriously as—? i know my body's legit, my fantasy. Prodigal femme, i smoky eye, nipple clip, Coney Island chic a way through, use language to say who i am.

i like my body best when it confuses itself, when exits flip & become a way in. Do you think my tongue is butch or femme? top or bottom? cis—? Would you find my breath warm, my forearms soft, thighs welcoming, all stretch marked & hairy?

Spit in my mouth if you're kind   & interesting.

O many gendered me, abundant as we've always been. The inner child knew without words—my gender is.   i do.

#poetics

The world is full of cuties, many of them poets & dancers. Joke's on everyone i guess.

May was all meadow light burst through strands, everything cusping coalesce & slip. Late of the month i landed in love, my feels, renewed— the same old colors more vivid more pop, rose quartz about my neck & every song ever written verse chorus bridging me to you,

staring across a table, you with your face in the rain. Pplx catch glimpses

of each other. Pplx garden gaps. The silence is gay the dashes too my lipstick & ruby slippers their dykey flannel denim on wool. We pass each other apples crunchy peanut butter on knives pour over morning sun life the rain the ravens blackbirds & jays long walks over yellowed leaves to the bagel place the bookstore the drum school where S teaches two kids paradiddle. It makes me blush—

women loving women—a miracle. Everyday is so much asking. We waltz in late to *Hustlers* having driven circles round the lot, just as J Lo drapes Constance Wu in fur, shares a smoke & it's the sweetest thing. Mid-movie you grab us slushies. i think *girl yr my man-them* & swoon a bit inside—their trench coat jacket their messy hair, my floral dress & the breeze where femininity dangles—tidal, open, all my salt sucked out to sea.

What do i want but so many versions of the world? What does anybody?

For a time S texts me every night at 4am eastern from the PNW. i wake like clockwork or just before, hold hands across a continent.

You know what really roils my marmalade? Relationship hierarchies. Gender conflated with member founding decent neighborhoods, senate seats & sound schooling. What if a person isn't woman, isn't man, isn't a perfect fucking catch bring home to the colony?

Someone screen a film with gay poly pods, thriving…

Later i try Lex, Tinder, feeld, cruise Grindr (for a moment, again)— *ISO TRANS FEMMES & OR ANYBODY WHO DOESN'T STRICTLY GENDER THEIR PARTS, PETS, SHOE SIZE, WAISTBANDS, ISO CURIOUS CONSENSUAL HOT AF PLAY, DTF, DFW, NO HITTING UNLESS ASKED, NO SHAME EVER LIKE NORMALIZE GAS, DON'T BE A DICK BUT LOVE GIRL DICK & DATE ME IN THE LIBRARY BUTT RAVISH ME IN QUIET i'm READING THIS FUCKING BOOK #AQUARIUSSUN #VIRGORISING #CAPMOON #CAPVENUS #SORRY*

Like i think i'd fuck me but also have my doubts.

Poetry bottom, spoony, gets switchy but that's a stretch, will fetch you breakfast, braid your hair, bring your phone when you leave it by my bed, listen & check in & check in & check. Fantasy—that's someone asking if i'm okay.

(blush emoji)

i come from where i come, love the distance, the reaching, perhaps as much as anything, will lose myself & forget, come back & beg a lyric tears the world ajar, soars a sec then slams aground, says *look at this, none of it is fine.*

Also, i want joy. It's absurd—

every day i turn a look, swipe right, give a like, text my friends in the anthropocene, each thread leading farther away from yesterday, smothered in feels, vibing for vibes, my thoughts banal with sidewalk texture, traipsing up & down & back & up the same handful of blocks which, to my eyes, must be the most gorgeous blocks of any blocks in any city anywhere. There's

kids trudging slow behind their mothers, distracted by gadgets & tricksters on wheels, seeing me now, confusion eyed—*boy? girl? whatever, okay!* There's all these

brownstones & brick facades, weathered & mortared by hands evoked ghostly. Remember? real folks brought their bodies down, laid every timber, each slate & brick so that

inside, someone could unpack groceries—vegetables & salted fish, pineapples coconuts yellow watermelon things i've never seen or named, cooked in every corner of every block in all the world—prepped & chopped, stirred & simmered, spiced, ladled & plated up—kitchens hoary with wisdom, a generation for every pinch in the pot. It's true pplx get hungry, start fucking all dirty, sweaty with kink, hard & or tender, silicone toy vibrators like microphones make ya sing—with leather, lots of leather, maybe vegan leather strap-ons & knots tied tight, consent so heady the tiniest hairs on the ridge of an ear check in—*Hello! Are you okay? i'm okay too yeah gooood*—hot hot hot & nobody gives a shit whether the person or persons their sleeping with are fat or bony or differently abled, what appendages they have or don't, what pronouns stick to their frames atm or if there's shit blood cum piss smearing the ceiling, so long as they're safe & seen, fucked deep down & good &

do i romanticize? Yes,

every block homes its violence, its own wellsprings & hydrants unspool-
ing. Hang out, eyes open, come come come & see

i learn slow—moving, talking, listening in—tongue tones & potlucks with friends, sick aunts, ailing moms, neighborly chats run over run over. L & i paint each other's nails on the stoop. A roommate's home sick. Momma braids her child's hair. Friends heal from top surgery, cozy with Netflix & stew, screens droning, pplx working through, budgeting weeks, pills or no—ket, coke, green & crystals, advice from the deck as i wonder

if half-bent sunflowers see me, strutting down Dean like autumn runway style, twenty-first century roses blooming to beautify the carbon of a nation unwilling to witness gloaming. i think back several springs when i finally learned to listen—all there was was Rihanna & the Adhan at evening-tide, Sabbath sirens wailing Friday, sticky night come play. Sundays i'd spin *A Love Supreme*, eavesdrop heaven figuring SOURCE is everywhere—from gum-squashed pavement to sky ever-azure, glitter eye peak *Euphoria*, waiting on the B65 to beam me up.

i'm at my best when really feeling it   veins tendons sinews my arteries & gassy tubes—just a curly-headed bucktooth femme, my girl dick, self-worth & fuckability a tangled up rune lyric love poem for mystery, for everything that ever saw sky & said *i don't know how to do this.*

Wandering alone, weather adoring, past block parties & chickens grilling, chairs among gingkoes & folks stooping, flower boxes & plastic gnomes, Jesus Christ & Mickey Mouse, past skateboards & short shorts check my skorts & schools out, *lemonade* & *long time*, drip pigeon shit, who knows? i get a bit nervous come seasonal shift—can't hide a dress beneath a long coat, can't hide shaved legs in these jorts or let my tenor clap back to *hey gorgeous* sans risk. It's revealing, bodies going glitch on main, my hoops & curls & curls for days like damn i look good— everybody looks so good i—

Bed-Stuy. Do i belong here? No / can't say, wasn't home elsewhere either, even among what made me. What can ever bring things even? Violence keeps it all in check, keeps me keeping & kept where

This is not an answer. My poem asks & asks &

Fast-forward, Riis Beach—waves & babes now take to streets, bridges blocked, city hall sleeping bag pride(s) reclaimed—June July rewind, bb. *Brunch can wait.*

Joy, that's pplx—jams & rooftop reads, hearts full with much at stake. Close to home there's B's old place, Super Food & Brower Park this way. i seltzer, grateful for friendships that tether. How nice it'll be to walk, post-pandemic, shop junk, cruise shoes, up & down Fulton for screen prints & rotis, chill in the plaza when weather warms.

On Pacific i see W walking K—his big lab retriever friend with huge paws who sees me, pees & it's the sweetest thing. We talk dogs & fire trucks rolling up last night, talk windowsills on my building collapsing & the questionable reparation, talk cigarettes & O look—there's the super, T, & my wild roomy C, pruning her garden of sunflower & vine, tomato & plum, datura sprigging, nary a sign of sewer leaks below.

We are neighbors & we talk, human & we struggle—laugh too, dig similar foods, hate landlords with vigor, say *fuck the ruling classes fuck the president* like good pplx do. i bet we're ashamed of things we've said or done or failed to, but also, occasionally, can be like *hey—remember that thing you tried, even though you were scared & you crushed it anyway?* something like that, in whatever words we use with our different tongues, different dialects, this language we share that betrays us all differently & still—

sometimes, late at night, i bet we shoot up in bed, thinking one day we'll take our last breath & will it hurt? will we be scared? will it be violent? will we be still? will any of this mean anything & will anyone we love be there?

We keep speaking till words run low, go separate ways to separate worlds that perhaps become less separate the more we keep talking. It's complicated—not rosy but a mess, tracks violent passages—your neighbors your block the earth you share.

Somewhere in space-time W's pplx come from Africa. europe, mine. Here we are, colliding in america, P Street adjacent, garbage & poo, rats clamoring beneath the tree on our verge, the places we call home.

Evening & the sky is lowing, night slipping hir blue bird shell. See us, our many we's, suture bound in deep ecologies—as though from hemlock we had drunk. You be you babe & i'll do me—meet here & there along the way. Still,

it's like why go to Bushwick or Bowery, chase Berghain sunrise for subs bassy bassy, pack fogged out basements or Appalachian clearings just to dance when my neighbor across P Street 'll happily drag a speaker to the lip, crank Commodores, crank Chic, crank Teddy P love TKO & all the best jams?

Baaaaaaabe, just gabba gabba gimme the loudest fastest dumbest shittiest EDM out here & i'll sway my hips, bounce my little belly beneath a two-dollar halter, let myself be strange in a sea of strangeness, try & want my own body first.

i think back on April, the before times & me, thirsty for showers, getting feisty in my bedroom to the Jesus & Mary Chain—cut sleeves, cedar sticks blazing, everyone in the world still alive—how i caught myself catching me in vanity, like *maybe this is your season to be slutty bb, to not hold on so tight.*

Even in these times a person can be happy you know.

life trance hacks
mourning sound

Where a mushroom ends or begins is hard to tell. Is it in the trees,
the fruiting body, or the underground webs?
And how easily it can seep into soil and pores and make them
mushroom-like, too!
It is something so many humans try to forget,
the fact of our porosity.
—Amanda Monti

There is more to be learned from wearing a dress for a day
than there is from wearing a suit for a lifetime.
—Larry Mitchell

blue azaleas

Blue azaleas climb skyward all around.
i close my eyes & they could replace me.

So many ways to body & i am human—watch
me swallow nails, bind my needs to stone, sink

ultramarine. Believe me when i say the world
takes who wishes. Post-reading, stroll Washington

Square, spliff the dark paths & wonder
if poetry's still got space for loneliness.

i'm saying languages are fading, everything
going extinct, but all i can think of is cold

gathering itself on my stoop, how i want to play
the little spoon, would you please hold me,

honey tender through raven dark? i dream futures,
sometimes a we & we are happy there—a garden,

bed on the floor, moon duvet & occasional feet
in the ocean—but i need portraits to believe.

Pardon me, i'm turning azalea. i'll step out,
count cracks in the walk, adjust for breakage.

You are so brave, my friends say. *You are a boy*
in a dress, says everyone else. i say i'm afraid

all the time, of alone & being question mark,
what people can do with just their eyes & more.

Don't mind me, i'll revert—rib, cobalt, clay,
whatever's easiest. People want sense

but that's not sensible. How hard we work
at not being so. i'm lapis, something inevitable.

Stay if you want, window unlatched,
bowls of cherries between the sheets.

the way we get by

Counting calories, disassociating during sex.
   Saying yes when what we mean is
      when what you want is
         when nightshade numbs nostrils, powder

      & breath. Whatever your pleasure, take it—
   now subtract by half. Who am i
to deny it? Pills crushed, back-throat tickle,
brown liquor kick & blood bluing veiny

the more supine we get. There can only be so many
   the Ones—so many it-girls & queer celebs,
      stable, gassed up, new bodies to market to
         What makes me tender but this sense we share

      of lack? Shutting my eyes on Riis last Sunday,
   in the boombox blur of gay boy strut,
  i imagined there was enough for us
& before me lay the fullness

of the sea. Everyday someone tries to feed me
   cake, says you're asking for it, threatens
      to bash face, mansplains the body in & out
      of being, compounds many

to one. i want this white world flayed,
    floundered to muck. May the muck
  receive me, the plastic pass freely through
the belly of a bird, her tubes unknotted

& loosed of debt. Tomorrow, some WE will gather
  in the plaza crying never say yes when
    what you mean is FUCK THIS! i'm headed there
    from many directions—land & sea, a stolen

    estuary, stolen hillside, cul-de-sac & car park
  with basketball net. Violence holds it all
  in place, keeps me keeping & us kept, a state
of insurmountable owing. Listen—that's ENOUGH

i say—eat what you want & will to live, take my hand
  & know me deep, splatter gush as night
    unsettles, moss about our ankles like lips
      gliding north a wrung of clavicle,

    moonlight spooling curves
  like drenched dogs dilating with heat.
  If we get real good at loving ourselves,
do we get really good at loving each other?

i mean damn differences & exalt them,
  top to bottom, cop free & free your mind
    bb, does it work like that? Apoplectic morning
      pouring musk in our gourds—the two of us,

now three, four, fifty, a hundred hundred
loaves & fishes, red veiled yolk queens
run kink deep for joy, punk-ass chains
hickeyed round our necks in a fellowship

of thorns. When i say you of course i mean me,
mean not not-you, we halfway-to-it-girls
gathering abundance while mistaking
seven seas for salt. Knowing pain, seek

NO PAIN, yet build by any means—the fire
-wicked bottle breaking glass, a trowel poked glory
hole tilled in mud—the how of our love, caloric,
igniting, what i always mean to say when wavering.

adjacent lines

The poem exposes some piece of me—maybe it's my liver, a hangnail left thumb, mole or dimple or bacteria swirl in the gut. Associations in the body appear as closed loops, though not only—its everybody's inside, some part of me is you & how many parcels of each does it take to build an I, already plural from the get?

Here's the romance of friendship, ekphrasis of eating ice cream & dumbly holding hands, girls lined defiant top the barricades of wrath. You think to yourself *I like this line or at least where it's going,* follow thoughts across the page, left right left in this colony language but who knows—so many directions & means of approach. A text authors its own gaze(s) but in this case how would you know unless you know me, cum inside to taste my many?

The thought occurs (unbridled, on speed) that umbilical is close to imbecile, as in *why would you sever yourself from source?* What Jesus realized as they screamed, crossed, or conversely, how i imagine a dervish or breaker might feel, whirling the blessed day gone.

Plants grow on my sill & i place clippings in water to root. We follow the line till it drops, breaks, can hold itself no longer. A bough, covered with snow. Never was i ever a tree but maybe—that's how the next line goes. Root, sap or thread may bind us, something sticky at least—lusty though more than just—melancholic with the ways language fails.

Happiness being no more obtuse than bruise or boredom or restfulness once one quits, having upturned every stone.

i say unironically *i'm alive & it's going okay*, ever in pursuit of adjacent lines. Something about feelings i've yet fully felt, leafing my savings for another green eighth. Time is long, measured in labor sales or frolicking fucks, though rest assured one makes for better poems. The radio's all pop & i dig it—baby don't leave me now where did our love go—like a prayer, words tumble my gorges.

Let's meet at the confluence by nightfall, blue river, tongues tipsy with heat & cellular light. A closed loop is not a body, the body a hole to fill, filled by many—

Say more, you think, *who knows where this all might go.*

Michael Stipe, Douglas Martin & me

get stoned around midnight, listen to *Monster*, read *Outline of My Lover*.
i always kill my darlings & they always cycle back. See? i'm not the only

one who loves you, Michael—crabgrass baritone, south of my youth
swamped kudzu & you—the first voice to queer me, lay me low.

Did you know from the get we shared more than punk & jangle,
that gardening's best done cloaked? "Tongue" isn't my favorite

song but it's sexy, not like Kurt like Michael—glamorous sinew
& dangerously smart. i've tried many times to write poems for you.

In my head they're all cicadas, clicking meter. They got ice
-cold swimming holes in May, nude queers splashy under star-bands

dreamy—oak, pine, creepy clapboard sheds, shotgun houses
& trestles damp with dew, the locomotive din of my youth-bound

room, mandolins drawn as small towns surrender to New York.
It's comforting when you laugh at Dr. Seuss, mumbling paths through verse.

Honestly reminds me of my not-boy girlhood, spun like happy people
do. i even dig you aloof, as Douglas has you—beautiful, fragile, in your own

head we are, i am—us gentle ones drenched in moon-full recall.
People always speculate—strung out on bennies, HIV, bi in hi-fi

& stuff everybody knows. Once i had a boombox, tape deck & laser,
Automatic the first disc i owned. Fine—that & *The Spaghetti Incident?*

but we remember what serves, don't we? Now here's three of us,
same city, 20th century sleeping & this new one waking rough.

i could go anywhere just knowing that you love me

I.

morning upsurge—cobblestones
& Stolpersteine
i recall brass in the walk
a beautiful mosque, pagoda
under construct

field, a flat expanse
control tower looming
the distance—
M takes me
to their garden plot
we pluck sage

dried like husk
chip of Berlin wall
in storefront, brash &
lingering—what happens is

imperceptible. M, sweetly
elfin, prax twig medicine & drums
speaks a dreamy German. i notice
how morningsun colors
their bowl blond
as they see me—

new dress, merino wool
U2 arrive timely
& time's so lazy here.

II.

Here's B & i last January—the two of us shopping at Other Nature, buying butt plugs, cock rings & lube—winding our way through Kreuzberg, its bomb-flecked facades front lit, block after block cross the gloaming Landwehr waters, towards a corporate Kino in garish Potsdamer Platz. Inside we sit separate, watch *Knives Out*, root for Marta claim her due from the wretched Thrombey clan.

Good times—Marta wins—but what i want to tell you is how that night, walking, we traced a route of one-time wall, talked intimate ledges, our lives dependent on holding—but onto what? where? who? O walls we abide in thick of families, nations, notions of being set to stone, tenuous borders, bodies & homes—

What would our ancestors think? we ask, speaking around the table next morning. How would they see us—Black, white, bodies like question marks cuddling, sharing coffee & poems, Nutella & muesli, a once-unfathomable friendship held supple—intention & breath forever stained in new world vile—haunted flesh sewn fear & map? Later, we're two

friends warming round a garbage fire, outdoor flea, resting with work-ers, swapping sweaters, buying rings of bent spoon wrap our fingers —bellies full of warmth.

III.

i need a sky spread-legged
& slutty as me—
turquoise clot reigning over
every dyke, mixing sweat
& fountain jet, Washington Square
ever extra, our pinups holding
hands, taught nipple clip
hysteric—
this Sapphic cavalcade.

Gays in summer—
not for nothing
the ocean throws us.
Name a piece of earth
that really wants
our raunchy thirst
queer, utopic. It's silly
i get teary as the Velvets play—
ugly cry, hanker for soft drugs
& nameless sex, Coney Island
beaches where S & i make
dances, stoney baloney
in August night.

IV.

The problem hinges on a biblicality.

Whose keeper am i if not yours,
mine, another's? i keep wondering—
who becomes a we?

V.

B says the gays are outta control
says i'm literally mad at you
for sending me that Fiona Apple song
texts a meme Tops Are Replenishing
the Planet, Healing, implying Bottoms
to blame. i answer with eye roll
emoji, triple heart emoticon. So & so
laughs at a comment.

During quarantine everyone is
horny. i mean hungry. i mean same.
Zoom zoom zoom, DM.
Surveillance is outta control
but O—i wanna be seen!

VI.

In loss one loses things—whole pplx so nakedly absent. What i long for most is to move through worlds with you, doing nothing & accomplishing little, sitting here, humming jingles to your bench-side ear, peering down the lunch pail at rough drafts, the resilience of chapped hands, your gushy eyes—

VII.

Living for it—
the way i feel when waking, the neighborhood sounding off,
how folx down Pacific will swing by Super Food Town,
clog entire aisles dancing Music City tunes. It must be dream work
makes a morning so sweet. All things cyclical—not plague, but a poem
    & relation.
L & i linger—spooning, giggling, our tiny bodies drip.
i could go anywhere just knowing that you love me,
that loads of friends & neighbors stayed on—in Ridgewood & Bushwick,
Bed-Stuy, Crown Heights, Boone Fork & both Villages—in Macau,
Berlin, Seattle, Hong Kong, even Oakland. Some went west
with the reddening clouds & i'd like the sky to stay open

flirt a little longer with all of them.

selfie

i'm cutest when my hair's real poofy, soft
ringlets rising inches off my head, coiling
like filaments in a flittering bulb. i take a selfie,
take fifteen selfies, work light in the stairwell
like i'm obsessed with it, go to my room
& masturbate, text wet pics & wave emojis
posing like the trans futanari femme i wish
i was—who can't stop minding their phone
long enough to attend a poem, read the tenant's
union notes, type actual words to L.

In flat screen glow i catch myself staring
& with each angle spiral low—all *you look hot
AF bb* straight to *that cock of yours is shameful*
zero to sixty in less than ten—calling in questions
of fuckability & worth. Elsewhere my mother
lays dying, cancer wrapped around her
like garlands on a wreath. i wonder where
i'll go to mourn her, sifting through
batches of family pics   magic shows,
fossil kits, Lincoln logs, pick-up-sticks, buck
tooth baby curl skipping stones over surge
years like they're mutable—calm & flat.

It's been weeks since my body's been touched
by hands other than mine—rub one off
on the reg, sure, & not that it gets old,
just lonely & frightening at the end of a world.
Like, how not to hate your selfish self,
feeling mopey, mid pandemic, short schleps past
city morgues spill to freezers parked in the street?

A slides in my dm's, says my skin looks great—so
why do i feel dim, waxy like butcher paper wrapping
red meat, waiting on hands to render me soppy,
something approaching living, more than just raw
beef? i am alive—what's your secret?
Seems venal, narcissistic, even needy, snapping
nudes for nobody in midst of global W-T-F.

My heart's like this pizza slice i clocked, dropped
cheese side up on Dean last Tuesday—hello flies,
hello footprint, hello all ye varmints of the world!
Just keep eating—eat & sleep & drink water often,
try loving yourself, if not this fate.

a dream is want at its wildest

for Sophie Xeon

Look at all us making poems at the end of the world.
Some things bear repeating—like how's your heart?
like a body is something liminal, even as it withers.
Imagine a dance floor—lovers & friends bump you can't even
move, shocks of mood & flash-strobe heat eviscerating what hurts
inside. You hold someone in sight, aura, endearment
as others hold you, smell of sour patch, armpits
& grind, concrete, Club Mate, liquor piss, floored—
everything unlatched at the hips. A poem means
shit if it won't cum in yr face, swash like hungry ocean
all spit soak & tongue. You've friends to look to & seeds
to tend, even as things feel hopelessly wrecked.

Every passing could be mine, could be yours, could be
someone out here chillin' with books & spliffs, lukewarm
in candle-drenched tub, sans sleep minus pills or
songs on repeat, maybe staring up a moon one clear
Jan night. Who isn't hungry for a closer look? Begrudge
no body. A poem should rave itself raw, warm like streaks
of jizz cutting lines down legs, coax moans in tones
never dreamt you'd reach—deep triangular wave loops
all acid plastic neon squelch, round every sweaty torso
in the rooms we once made—nothing but lust & motion,
this relentless reaching towards.

No one belongs forever & i'm just some sad girl in curls
with wondering eyes saying *c'mere i got something*
to tell ya. People say you can't change the world, only yourself
inside it. Wanna swing by tonight? Let's get high & spin
records—i got *Interstellar Space* & *Neu! '75*, got *Oil of*
Every Pearl's Un-Insides topped by *The Hounds of Love*.
A dream is want at its wildest & so can we—inarticulate bc
not yet, un-translatable bc always in trans-. The real poem
says i miss you, adore you i can't wait to see you again,
writes a world & you're still here, wishes ya hadn't
got sick, got sad, died. The line, free of hubris, straight
up like times are hard enough make your heart sink
where it hangs. Like a beat dropping. Like an angel,
descending, then rising back up.

* * *

wound / vision

The boss bitch is not my sister, not the nation & she ain't my mother.
i say i'm a traveler not a conqueror, nor am i passive either.
There are bodies yearning inside me & we vibe. At the secret rave
in Prospect dark the dancing's erratic post so much sick.
We take poppers off PrEP(py) gays who in before times
sneered at my wholly repurposed cock. Imagine utopia,
disability informed. i like to come off loose & unsettled,
as if counter narratives negate all complicit. Doesn't
everyone want these drugs, these kinks, these particular beats
& wood? A vision is just that—whoever's & yours & y'all talk.

i fuck myself often as body allows, deep as i can & a little
plus. The erotic's a channel to what i know i don't yet know—
shy inside, bend me over, help me understand anything.
If utopia is ecological, speech acts sown & spun,
what'll we squeeze from the gut rot of capital?
You see a wound is just that—it's a vision.
A ziploc full of mangos from a woman in the tunnel. Subway,
she elder. The total ecstasy of fruit in summer. The pleasures
of juice stick fingers to tongue. A poem says look up look sideways
see the web laced fierce. Yes i'm naïve & a poem is anything.

Try quiet or talk all the time who cares. Herbert Von King
& Covid summer—babes at a distance, squat in the bush, weed-
splayed ballpark all a league of their own—it's small things
get you over. Take holy mother Sylvia's big plush bear or every pic

of pups & Arca. Take Beverly Glenn-Copeland any morning, dawning
my paint-splattered Malcolm X-Betts. i wear lockets & smocks
& denim on wool, tie-dye with rhinestone or hoops. Crushes, sweet
crushes EROTICS OF SNUGGLE scribbled in spiral, all caps
like Juliana Huxtable. Sometimes pop songs jet me outta time,
mostly reify it. O nostalgia, dreary of cards—here is the life

i've lived. Cup, coin, staff, sword, the dog doesn't fall it's the Fool.
A wound, friend, is just that. In the city i hear everything.
Lie—i lift what's mine to hold. Out in the street an I joins we
& we march, shout, crouch & lock arms you you you & you—
INTIFADA INTIFADA <clap clap clap> caps again like June Jordan
& the voice in my throat goes gravel, set to gut by blood-bound
ancestors traipsing where they should not go. Me—i'm pavement,
step step step over stolen ground, hello. i don't think
the world lets people be good & so we do what we do,
we do it here, in the world.

notes

The proem **open letter utopia** was written (mostly) on the U-Bahn in response to a screening of Dagmar Schultz's film *Audre Lorde: The Berlin Years 1984 to 1992* at Lichtblic-Kino, Berlin.

ecologies

Epigraphs from this section come from Hurston's *I Love Myself When I Am Laughing...And Then Again When I Am Looking Mean and Impressive* (Feminist Press) & Mayer's *The Desires of Mothers to Please Others in Letters* (SplitLevel / Nightboat Books).

so the maggots know references Stylites, bog people, Arthurian legend, Joan of Arc, Emily Dickinson, the brambles of southern Appalachia, etc. i've lifted the line "light like the life i'm in" from Bernadette Mayer's poem "What Babies Really Do" & used it in **these cadaverous times**. In **mother, mother**, "Crossing the Bar" is a poem by Tennyson, while "Sunflowers" is Mary Oliver's. **Lonely mountain town** incorporates lyrics & images from the song "Tom Dooley," in which the titular character murders Laura Foster in the hills of western North Carolina. References are also made to Andrew Wyeth's painting "Christina's World" & an imagined reclamation of Tammy Wynette's "Stand By Your Man." **sweet poem** calls up a scene from *Amélie* & **wild geese with transsexuals & acid** trips through troubled memories alongside Oliver & SOPHIE.

field jar

Epigraphs from this section come from Benjamin's *One-way Street and Other Writings* (Penguin) & Coleman's *Bathwater Wine* (Black Sparrow Press).

The term field jar is borrowed with gratitude from Andrea Rexilius' book *New Organism: Essais* (Letter Machine Editions). My poem, **field jar**, makes reference to KitKat, a club in Berlin, as well as the u.s. presidential election of 2016 & neighborhoods in both Berlin & Brooklyn. **sunday morning malaise** is, in part, thinking with the work of Andrea Abi-Karam. **body clocks** was written in conversation with Etel Adnan's piece "To Be In A Time of War" from *In the Heart of the Heart of Another Country* (City Lights Books). *Music for Airports* (Polydor Records) is an album by Brian Eno. Another Country is a used bookstore, Silver Future, a queer bar. Both are in Berlin & both appear in **year of the rat**. Rosa Luxemburg (perhaps) rests at Zentralfriedhof Friedrichsfelde, or the Garden of the Socialists.

terrarium bimbo pop

Epigraphs from this section come from Acker's *Great Expectations* (Penguin), "Kill Me," from the record *Any Shape You Take* (Saddle Creek) by Indigo De Souza & one of my beloved friend's many truisms.

towards an economy of anal delights does not convey a precise Marxist analysis (it's just a poem don't @ me). Riis Beach, featured here & elsewhere, is a queer beach in Queens. **ants on a log** plays fast & hot with Eileen Myles' "Peanut Butter" (*Not Me*, Semiotext(e)) & lines from Miguel Gutierrez's self-published chapbook *Blowjobs, I like him, my friend is dead*. The poem emerged from the Anchoress Syndicate's 2021 workshop "My Smutty Valentine: Queer Kinships and the Poetics of Smut," hosted online by the Poetry Project. **Like any woman's penis** references actor Hunter Schafer, specifically in her / their role of Jules in the smash hit HBO melodrama *Euphoria*, as well as makeup supplier Sephora & Rihanna's brand, Fenty, not to mention *The New Fuck You: Adventures in Lesbian Reading* (Semiotext(e)). The addressee of **red dirt garden goth girl** is none other than THE Diane from Andrea Lawlor's novel *Paul takes the form of a mortal girl* (Vintage), a character i endlessly crush on despite the judgements of literally everyone. This poem also references the "long dark blues" of Jason Molina / Songs: Ohia / Magnolia Electric Co.,

Dolly Parton's "Jolene" & film *9 to 5*, Laurie Foster & Tom Dooley (again), Gillian Welch's "Wrecking Ball," Garth Brooks's "The Dance," & Lucinda Williams's *Car Wheels on a Gravel Road* (Mercury Records). Yellow Jackets refers to gas station speed & Cheer Wine is a southern VA / NC regional soda. Bojangles & Waffle House, well those are places you eat. **nicotine libidinal** is a poem wherein the author / fan speculates (perhaps misguidedly) about Kurt Cobain's gender while paying respects to their significance. The poem references Nirvana's performance at the 1992 Redding Festival, the records *In Utero* & *Incesticide* (Geffen Records) & the porous spellings Kurt used re name. Courtney Love / Hole's jam "Doll Parts" also makes an appearance, as does Neil Young's "Sleeps With Angels" & Kurt's love for Aerosmith. **every pearl's un-insides (feat. poppers + feels)** was commissioned for the Poetry Project Newsletter's *SOPHIE Remembrances*. Writing the piece consisted of taking poppers, smoking weed & writing along to every track of SOPHIE's *OIL OF EVERY PEARL'S UN-INSIDES* (Transgressive / Future Classic / MSMSMSM). Rooney Mara's character from the film *Carol* cameos in & inspires the narrator of **desire goes nowhere but somewhere sometimes.** Larry Kramer's lecture references his speech at the Queer Liberation March & rally in Central Park, summer of 2019. That same Diane pops up again here, too. Rachel refers to the trans woman Lou Reed dated in the '70s & Coney Island Baby is a reference to his album of the same name. Doughnut Pub is a doughnut bar i like to frequent on 14th St. & STAR House refers to the house, operated by the Street Transvestite Action Revolutionaries, that gave shelter & support to queers, sex workers, basically the faggots & their friends. Marsha P. Johnson & Sylvia Rivera were the house mothers. John Varvatos is a "rock & roll clothier" located (at the time of writing) in the former site of CBGB, downtown on Bowery. Cubbyhole is a lesbian bar in the West Village. The Factory was Andy Warhol's studio / home base & "Andy" is him while "Valerie" is Valerie Solanas, his would-be assassin & founding mother of SCUM (Society for Cutting Up Men). David Wojnarowicz was an artist, writer, activist & visionary. *Julieta* is a film by Almodovar, *The Handmaiden* by Park Chan-wook & Sunshine Cinema was a theater on Houston. Sheridan Square is a small park in front of the Stonewall Inn & Happyfun Hideaway is a queer bar in Bushwick.

true blue uncanny valley

Epigraphs from this section come from Howe's *Night Philosophy* (Divided Publishing) & Adnan's *Night* (Nightboat Books).

The line about Adorno is based (loosely) in both his work & conversations with my friend, B. 1619 refers to the year in which the first enslaved Africans arrived in what would become the united states, 1492 to the onset of european genocide against the Indigenous Pplx of the so-called "new world." Holocene is a geologic era & Will Smith joins the poem from the film *Independence Day*. Lex, Tinder, feeld & Grindr are dating apps. *A Love Supreme* (Impulse!) is an album by John Coltrane, duh. *Brunch can wait* was a chant hollered by queers at oblivious outdoor diners during the Queer Liberation March, NYC, 2020. "gabba gabba etc." is a chant used by Ramones. There's a lot of references in this poem but these are some of the main ones.

life trance hacks mourning sound

Epigraphs from this section come from Monti's *Mycelial Person* (Vegetarian Alcoholic Poetry) & Mitchell's *The Faggots & Their Friends Between Revolutions* (Nightboat Books).

blue azaleas was written after a reading by Anaïs Duplan at McNally Jackson. **the way we get by** is inspired by June Jordan's fierce-as-fuck poem "Intifada Incantation: Poem #8 for b.b.L." Michael Stipe was the singer for R.E.M. & Douglas Martin is an author / artist / teacher who wrote a book that's maybe about him called *Outline of My Lover* (Nightboat Books). **Michael Stipe, Douglas Martin & me** references several R.E.M. records & songs while striving for a queer lineage connecting the three titular characters. Kurt Cobain & Guns N' Roses cameo. The Stolperstein in **i could go anywhere just knowing that you love me** refer to cubic, brass plagues bearing the names of pplx murdered during the Holocaust outside their former places of residence in Berlin. The plaques are slightly elevated over the surrounding cobblestones, causing one to possibly trip &, therefore, make note. *Knives Out* is a film by Rian Johnson. Dean in **selfie** refers to a specific block in Crown Heights, Brooklyn. **a dream is want at its wildest** is a memoriam for SOPHIE & all those lost in the Covid-19 pandemic. The poem references albums by John Coltrane, Neu!, SOPHIE & Kate Bush & leaves me feeling devastated.

* * *

wound / vision, the closing bop, references diy queer parties i attended during the brief window of vaccination revelry, when largely able-bodied gays would come together & dance outside. There's a lot to say about this, but the poem wants to capture a bit of the joy shared before the lyric slams back to earth. Prospect & Herbert Von King are parks in Brooklyn. "a league of their own" references the film of the same name, a personal queer root. Sylvia Rivera was often pictured with stuffed animals, while Arca (a musician, trans cyborg type), if we are to believe instagram, clearly loves puppies. Beverly Glenn-Copeland is another brilliant, queer-of-gender musician & composer, while Malcolm X-Betts is a dancer, choreographer, writer, fashion designer & total Real One currently living & working in NYC. Julianna Huxtable is (another) queer af, multi-disciplinary artist (musician, writer, curator, thinker, etc.) who often writes in all caps & i'm again siting the aforementioned June Jordan poem, this time in reference to protests that took place outside of the isracli embassy in NYC, spring 2021.

Many thanks to the editors & readers at the following journals, where many of these poems first appeared:

Apogee, Nat. Brut, [PANK], Peach Mag, the Poetry Project Newsletter, the Rumpus & Tagvverk

gossip / gratitude

Nothing alone is useful, possible, desirable. All creation(s) are ecosystems, simultaneously discrete, multiple, an endless arching that can't be quantified or singularly named.

All of my words, thoughts, influences & inspirations, joys, anxieties, despairs-to-hopes & back again tether me like a rhizome, like mycelia, to the porousness of bodies & time. It is my communities that make me, re-make me, that hold & / or unravel me. We are done & undone, together. If life has any purpose, this ever-unfolding process must encompass it—generative, painful, tragic, jubilant, hilarious, despairing, sexy & full of tea. Any list of descriptors would necessarily be endless.

i am forever in happy debt to all the following folx & then some—whether (chosen) fam, community, lovers, beloveds, crushes, acquaintances, strangers at readings, on dance floors, the agitators, curators, cruisers, editors, classmates, co-workers, foils—all myriad forms of relation. Y'all make me human & i offer in turn my words—trinkets or junk, breath & embrace, however you like or want or need or don't. My love & need for poetry stems from my love of living in the worlds y'all are building. Thank you for seeing me & know i see you.

Adjua Gargi Nzinga Greaves, Ah-Keisha McCants, Alexis Wilkinson, Amber McZeal, Amanda Monti, Amra Causevic, Anaïs Duplan, Andrea Abi-Karam, April Freely, Arianne Ayu Alizio, Arti Gollapudi, Assad, Babay L Angles, Bayan Kiwan, Becca Bradley, Bernard Ferguson, Bri Frei, Bryanna Bradley, Caitlin Lynch, Capri, Carlo Antonio Villanueva, Catiriana Reyes, Celina Su, Cerridwen Elektra McQueen, Chia-Lun Chang, Chloe Blog, Claire Siesfeld, Couscous the Cat, David Glickman, effie bowan, Elliott Sky Case, Emma Wippermann, Emi Knight, Emily Skillings, Erica Dawn Lyle, Erika Hodges, Evelyn Sanchez Narvaez, frankie baker, Gabrielle Civil, Gala Mukomolova, Grace Caiazza, Forest Gray Yerman, Greer Dworman, Hannah Hirsch, India Lena González, Iris McCloughan, Isaac Poole, Ishmael Houston-Jones,

Izzi Rojas, J'royce Jata, Jack Petersen, Jaime-Jin Lewis, James Barickman, James Sherry, Janelle Tan, Jaz Sufi, Jiaoyang Li, Jill Preston, JinJin Xu, John Gutierrez, Joshua Deane McQueen, Josh Wizman, JUCK, jules onrubia, Kamelya Omayma Youssef, Kamikaze Jones, Karina Vahitova, Karisma Price, Kat Rejsek, Kay Gabriel, Kaya the Dog, Kimberly Alidio, Krystal Languell, Kyle Carrero Lopez, Landon Mitchell, Laura Henriksen, Layton Lachman, Leor Stylar, Lindsay Dula, Lindsey Briggs, Lindsey Hoover, Lissy Navantu, lix z, Lune Wynyard, Madeleine Ngoma, Malcolm X-Betts, mal profeta, marcus scott williams, Marie Hinson, Marion Spencer, Matthew Williams, Marley Trigg Stewart, Marti Irving, Max Puorro, Maya Simone, MC Hyland, Meghan Berry, Melissa Lozada-Oliva, Miguel Gutierrez, Mimi Gabriel, Nadra Mabrouk, Nafis White, Naima Yael Tokunow, Nancy Huang, nia nottage, Nikay Paredes, Olivia Hunt, Omotara James, Pamela Booker, Patricia Spears Jones, Patrick Loth, Peach Kandor, Penelope Bloodworth, Peter Oakley, Pheeyownah, Phoebe Osborne, Raha Benham, Rebecca Teich, Rider Alsop, Rina Espiritu, ro xiili särkelä-bassett, Ru (Nina) Puro, ryen blu ray heart, Ry Thomas, s lumbert, Sahar Romani, Sam Rush, Serena Marie Thomas, Sarina Romero, Sasha Debevec-McKenney, Seth Sullivan, Sheridan Riley, Silvi Naçi, Siobhan Butler, SoSoon, Stacy Szymaszek, Stephanie Acosta, Stephanie Young, stone tsao, Suzanne Goldenberg, Suzepuz, t'ai freedom ford, Talya Epstein, Tarika Wahlberg, Terrance Hayes, Tiara Roxanne, Tom Lloyd, Travis Reyes, tyler morse, Vida James, Viva Ruiz, Wazina Zondon, Wendy Xu, Wo Chan, Yanyi, Zachary Sussman, zaybra, Zefyr Lisowski.

i've been privileged to attend several institutions of so-called higher learning (to paraphrase Fred Moten, a classroom can be anywhere people gather in good faith to hash shit out) where i've been both a teacher's pet & terrible student. With that said, extravagant love & respect to all the peers i've shared workshops with, particularly in NYU's Creative Writing Program. Thank you for trusting me with your work & for your honesty & support re mine. Thank you for your solidarity & for engaging in the work of harm-reduction within institutions—a work that's ongoing. It's messy & complex—i've both benefited from institutional support (often monetarily & relationally) & have many misgivings.

A special shout out to Wo (*love is in the details*) & to Terrance, literally for everything (& that time you said *a poem just needs more good than bad*). To Omotara, for long nights laughing on the couch & April, for all you gave & are still giving. Thanks to Jay for teaching me line breaks & Janet, for refusing to let me fail.

Arisa White, Deborah Landau, Elitza Kotzeva, Emily Skillings, Dr. Herukhuti Williams, Janet Sylvester, Jay Wentworth, jayy dodd, Laurie Foos, Lucy Ives, Miguel Gutierrez, Richard Carp, Simone Kearney, Tan Lin, Terrance Hayes—in classrooms, workshops, zoom sessions, i'm forever grateful to have studied with you. Big love to my students at NYU & Goldwater Hospital for inspiration, revelation & grounding.

Thank you to the Anchoress Syndicate, Artist Space, Belladonna*, Brooklyn Poets, Crush Reading Series, Gibney & my LANDING cohort, Goddard College, the Home School cohort, Emerging Writers Reading Series, JUCK, NYU Berlin, NYU Creative Writing Program, the Poetry Project, Segue Reading Series, the Trans Oral History Project & Winter Tangerine. Extra, endless thanks & appreciation to the workers who keep these spaces safe(r), clean, lit, vital.

Thank you Nightboat—especially Caelan Nardone for such tender care with this text. Thanks to Kazim Ali, Stephen Motika & the labor of Gia Gonzales & Lindsey Boldt that made this book a tangible (arti)fact. Wild thanks to Somnath Bhatt for the hot cover design, to Elias Chen for the lavender images & HR Hegnauer for interior design.

Endless love to my NC fam—y'all have supported me in so many ways throughout the years, in friendship & collaboration. Big love to BK, Chris, Derek, Seth & Travis, who've taught me so much re collaboration.

For my mother's mother, Carolyn & her mother, Ruth—thank you for childhood dream-space, care & warmth. Emma, Ian, Mikki—thank you for seeing me, for following your truths, for the moments of joy we sometimes get to share. Thanks to the Loths for being my second family growing up. Thank you Elizabeth & Patrick, for your trueness & presence. Thanks to my father, for all the music.

Rebecca Teich. i love you so dearly. You're a home, a community, a forever-burst of brilliance. i'm so honored to move through this world in search of utopia, gay revelry & wildly extravagant typos as your friend. None of this exists without you. Texting as we speak.

Talya Epstein. Thank you for the title, for *Euphoria*, for ongoing, expansive friendship.

Miguel Gutierrez. Thank you for modeling what an artist can be, for being so endlessly open & always making me laugh.

Lissy Navantu. Thank you for showing me expansive love, for your patience & wisdom, your play, your immense generosity of care. You are my teacher, friend, lover, confidant & so much more that language cannot convey. Electricity. i love you forever!

Mom. i love you. i miss you & don't know what to do with all this absence. Thank you for reading to me, for putting books & poems in front of me, for encouraging my creativity. It is a great gift you have given.

Thank you chosen fam. Thank you reader. Bless all the faggots & their / our friends, holding it all together. Here's to healing, flirting with, dreaming—

everything & everyone is a teacher.

imogen xtian smith is a poet & performer. They live & work on Lenape lands / NYC.

Nightboat Books

Nightboat Books, a nonprofit organization, seeks to develop audiences for writers whose work resists convention and transcends boundaries. We publish books rich with poignancy, intelligence, and risk. Please visit nightboat.org to learn about our titles and how you can support our future publications.

The following individuals have supported the publication of this book. We thank them for their generosity and commitment to the mission of Nightboat Books:

Kazim Ali
Anonymous (4)
Abraham Avnisan
Jean C. Ballantyne
The Robert C. Brooks Revocable Trust
Amanda Greenberger
Rachel Lithgow
Anne Marie Macari
Elizabeth Madans
Elizabeth Motika
Thomas Shardlow
Benjamin Taylor
Jerrie Whitfield & Richard Motika
Arden Wohl

This book is made possible, in part, by grants from the New York City Department of Cultural Affairs in partnership with the City Council and the New York State Council on the Arts Literature Program.